The Handbook
of Stage Lighting

The Handbook
of Stage Lighting

Neil Fraser and Simon Bennison

THE CROWOOD PRESS

First published in 2007 by
The Crowood Press Ltd
Ramsbury, Marlborough
Wiltshire SN8 2HR

www.crowood.com

British Library Cataloguing-in-Publication Data
A catalogue record for this book is available from the British Library.

ISBN   978 1 86126 857 0

Frontispiece: From **Cinderella** by Serge Prokofiev for the Royal Ballet, Covent Garden.

The authors wish to acknowledge the generosity and skill of those directors, choreographers, designers, photographers, actors, dancers, singers and (of course) lighting designers mentioned in these pages, and thank them for allowing us to refer to and use pictures from their work. Particular thanks are due to the Royal Ballet, Monica Mason, Anthony Russell Roberts, Jeanetta Lawrence and Kevin O'Hare. Thanks also to the Royal Opera House, Geoff Wheel, Les Bone, John B. Read, John Charlton, all the lighting staff, and Martin Adams and the Linbury Theatre team. From the Yale School of Drama: Jennifer Tipton, William Warfel and Michael Yeargen. The cast of *The Price*, Nicholas Kent, Mary Lauder, Shaz McGee and all at the Tricycle Theatre, and Darren Hull Production LX for *The Price* West End run. All at the then Oxford Stage Company, Dominic Dromgoole, Sean Holmes and Anthony Lamble. For the Dundee Repertory Theatre, Dominic Hill, James Brining, Nicola Young and the casts of *Scenes from an Execution*, and *A Lie of the Mind*. Thanks also to Michael Hulls, Russell and Julia. And finally photographers Rob Moore, Asya Verzbinsky, Douglas McBride, Douglas Robertson, Selecon Lighting in New Zealand for raiding their picture library, and to Marie Southwood for patiently organizing this for us. A big thank you also to Cathy Marston for her generous contribution.

This book is dedicated to John Fraser and Harold Harrison.

Colour origination and pre-press by Bookcraft Ltd,
Stroud, Gloucestershire
Printed and bound in Singapore by CraftPrint International Ltd

CONTENTS

FOREWORD

I always feel that a well-lit restaurant makes food taste better. The experience becomes more pleasurable as a whole – naturally to the eye, but the feeling of well focused light on the skin is special, too. This also happens on stage: the first time you experience each transformed space is always exhilarating; it's the almost tangible beams of light cutting across you, and the concentration in the darkness of the theatre compressed into what is always a shorter-than-ideal time frame. As a dancer, the new environment wakens all your senses – you can almost smell it! On top of that there's always a little panic – somehow the floor is never where you expect it to be when you're caught in a shaft of sidelight. But this just acts as a call to the body to let the adrenalin flow, and soon it is finding imaginary cables to support you in the air.

As a choreographer, there's also a bit of a jolt in the first few moments when you see your work under stage light. In my collaborations with Simon Bennison we have usually planned the light's architecture well in advance together, but it's still a shock to discover what's revealed or concealed in your choreography. For those precious hours your eyes are working overtime to take in all the details, even the most subtle, of the images to which the players are exposed. In that moment I have two lines of communication: one, in hushed tones to Simon and the other, in a voice raised towards the stage, to my dancers. It's a brilliant exercise in multi-tasking and one that I throw myself into for the strictly defined period known as 'tech time'.

Good communication is of paramount importance in these rehearsals – although it is generally something that needs to be already established in the preparation stage. Often it's about a shared vocabulary. Experiment and patience are important, and sometimes the long route to a solution is as valuable as the quicker one. Diplomacy is a useful skill, although I feel it is best sometimes if you can break through the need for it and create a relationship based on a shared goal, on trust, honesty and openness, which is the route to the most rewarding collaboration.

It's so exciting for me to read this book, which is not only a wonderful guide to theatrical lighting, but also documents some of the wonderful journeys I have made in the creation of lighting for dance. I hope that the light it sheds on the sometimes dark and daunting process of collaboration will help others experience some of the fulfilment it has given us.

Cathy Marston
Director of Bern Ballet

INTRODUCTION

This book is about the process of creating lighting for live performance. Whether this performance is theatre, dance or opera, all the information that you need in order to create imaginative and visually effective lighting is here.

The first ten chapters of the book detail the principles and processes involved in creating a lighting design; the last four offer a series of case studies that take these ideas and use them in a number of carefully chosen, authentic and very real practical examples. In a unique way, therefore, the reader not only learns the techniques of lighting for the stage, but also gets to experience them in action.

Skill and craft in an industry such as theatrical lighting design can be confusing. Indeed, it has often been deliberately made to seem so, in order to create a sense of mystique around the art of staging a production – which, after all, is often about creating an illusion. This book endeavours to blow away this mist of obscurity, communicating in simple and straightforward terms an art form that has for many proved fascinating, exciting and, most importantly, immense fun. Any craft that deals with the stuff of life itself – light – should surely be nothing else!

Whether the action is acted, danced or sung (or a combination of all three), many of the things you need to know in order to produce fantastic lighting are much the same... but some are not. This book takes you through all the similarities and all the differences in fine detail, comparing the varied forms of theatrical performance along the way. Modern technology and equipment are explained, working methods and techniques made lucid, and creative and artistic concepts laid bare.

In this book the task of lighting a production is divided into ten vital steps, and these are followed by a number of detailed case studies of real productions (Chapters 11 to 14). The ten steps deal with an understanding of the role of the lighting designer and the distinct areas of the work involved in producing a great lighting design, and they are described, as much as is possible, in the chronological order in which they are likely to occur. These areas are as follows:

1. The job of the lighting designer: his place in the scheme of things.
2. The text: the originating material and how to study it.
3. The director (or producer: see below) and the designer: the development of the production style.
4. Theory: the ideas that lie behind the use of light on stage.
5. Meetings and discussions: the early stages of preparation.
6. Rehearsals: the gathering of information.
7. Creativity and inspiration: where the ideas come from.
8. The task in preparation: the process of working towards a lighting design on paper.
9. The equipment: the tools for the job.
10. The task in practice: the work in the theatre – rigging, focusing, plotting and cues.

Note: In opera, the person who runs the show is usually called the producer, whereas in all other types of production the term 'director' is used. To avoid confusion, 'director' is used for all cases throughout this book, except where opera is being discussed in isolation.

1 THE JOB OF THE LIGHTING DESIGNER

The starting point in any theatrical process has two strands: the material on which the finished product is going to be based, and the people who are going to create it.

In both cases what we have at the very beginning is quite simply an idea, or a collection of ideas – concepts and thoughts that need defining, refining and developing. In some cases, where a text is available, much of the work may appear to have been done in this area. However, even when the text of a complete five-act play is our starting point, there is still a serious amount of hard work to be done before anything can be put before an audience.

To be clear what it is we are talking about, here are some of the more obvious starting points that we may come across:

- a play text, for a dramatic piece;
- a text and libretto, for an opera or musical;
- a music text or the recorded music itself, to be used as the basis for a piece of dance;
- an idea or theme for the improvisation of a dance or drama;
- choreographic notation, for a previously mounted dance piece.

And below is a list of all those who may be involved with, and may contribute to, the artistic or creative decision-making process – the creative team:

- playwright
- composer
- librettist
- producer (*see* note on page 7)
- director
- musical director
- choreographer
- set designer
- costume designer
- lighting designer
- sound designer

Alongside these people, any number of management and technical departments work to realize their ideas; they are known collectively as the technical team:

- production management
- stage management

and the following departments:

- design
- scenic art
- costume
- wigs
- lighting
- sound
- construction
- props

This is, of course, a huge simplification, as any number of creative and artistic things may emanate from the so-called 'techies', whilst many

OPPOSITE:Warren Mitchell and Larry Lamb in The Price *at the Tricycle Theatre, London 2002.*

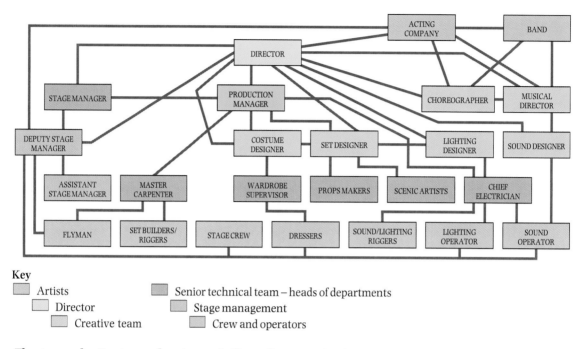

Key

Artists

Director

Creative team

Senior technical team – heads of departments

Stage management

Crew and operators

Theatre production team, showing main lines of communication.

a member of the group listed before them may fail miserably to come up with anything of any creative merit whatsoever – such is life!

However, for our purposes, a map of a typical large-scale production could be represented as in the chart above.

THE ROLE OF THE LIGHTING DESIGNER

As can be clearly seen above, the lighting designer has a creative role to play and also drives the needs of a complete technical department; however, he or she is rarely, if ever, the instigator of a piece. In fact, depending on what the piece is, and whilst they can be involved almost immediately, it can also be the case that they only become involved some time after the initial instigation.

For example, in the case of a new piece of choreography, a lighting designer may well be asked to attend the very first meeting in order to discuss what part the lighting is going to play in the finished production (although in the early

stages this may well, of course, remain only vaguely defined). On the other hand, a play may well be designed and in rehearsal before a lighting designer is asked to begin their work on the piece.

Whatever the case, what the lighting designer must do from the outset is become intimately acquainted with the product that has set the ball rolling – the impetus for the production. This is done in two main ways: by study and by discussion. The next section investigates how the lighting designer should approach studying the 'text'.

Originating a Dance Piece

It is clear from what has already been stated that of all dramatic staged productions it is the mounting of a piece of dance that differs the most from the other forms. More than anything this can be, and is particularly the case with, modern or contemporary dance, because the starting point is not via the written word or musical notation – and, as we shall see, because as part of the visual stage world of modern dance, lighting is often intended to provide a major aspect of what will be seen on stage, second only (perhaps?) to the performers themselves.

The Assistant Lighting Designer

In this book the job of lighting a production is assigned to the lighting designer, and to he or she alone. The role of an assistant to this figure is not featured. This is because whilst this role can surely enough exist in a production – indeed, any member of the team can have any number of assistants – it is always a difficult one to define. In fact it depends almost always on how the lighting designer (and the assistant) wish to define it. In any case, the work that they undertake still comes clearly under the collective banner of 'lighting design'.

To explain further: an assistant to the lighting designer could simply observe, or make useful artistic contributions. They could draw up the design, and undertake all communication with the technical team – indeed they could undertake all or a major part of the focusing and the plotting – or quite simply they may not. Therefore there are as many different variations of this role as there are people (paid and unpaid) to fill it!

In a similar way, a lighting design can be undertaken by a team – a joint project with two or more people. This is rare but not unknown and, once again, who does what depends completely on the team involved. Although also fairly rare, it is not unheard of for the set designer or director to add the role of lighting designer to their other duties. Naturally when this happens the role of the assistant lighting designer comes to the fore.

For the most part, in this book where the term 'lighting designer' is used, it can be considered as referring to one person or a team.

THE PRODUCTION WORK OF THE LIGHTING DESIGNER

Before looking in detail at the art of the lighting designer, it is worth first making sure that we have a clear sense of this art in the context of a whole production; we will then follow this process throughout this book. Put briefly, this is what a lighting designer does:

- gets to know well any material being used to originate the process (*eg* a text);
- meets and discusses the look and feeling that the production is going to have, particularly with the director and the designer;
- visits rehearsals and makes good notes about the placing and feel of the action of the piece;
- using knowledge of lighting theory and equipment, plans the lighting rig;
- draws up lighting requirements in the form of a plan, and makes many lists;
- communicates this to the technical team;
- is on hand to solve problems during rigging (even if on the end of a phone);
- focuses the rig;
- creates the lighting for each part of the production at a 'plotting session';
- refines and develops the lighting through both technical and dress rehearsals;
- attends the first night and enjoys the finished production (and/or leaves notes for the technical team if things still needed changing);
- keeps in touch with the production to make sure all remains well with the lighting;
- moves on to the next job!

To further clarify this process and its terminology: the lighting designer will produce a drawn document, often referred to as the 'lighting design', but in fact merely the means to provide the information to make sure the lighting rig is properly installed. The lighting design – if the term really has any meaning at all – remains for the most part in the head of the lighting designer right up until the point when it is created on stage. The drawn plan is used by the lighting team, copied and annotated with technical information specific to the venue (for example, circuit numbers), the equipment is then corralled, and finally put in place (rigged).

The lighting designer then directs the positioning of the equipment (the focus), and with the director (and often the designer) 'plots' the way the lighting will look for every specific moment of the production. After this 'plotting session', the piece goes into technical, and then dress rehearsal, it may preview, and then opens to a hopefully adoring public. The key terms are, therefore, in chronological order:

RIG FOCUS PLOT 'TECH' DRESS OPEN

There are, of course, any number of variations in this process, as shown by a typical production schedule (see illustrations below and opposite). A good example being the modern trend to incorporate the plotting into the technical rehearsal.

PRODUCTION SCHEDULE		Scenes from an Execution
Sat 17th	10.00 p.m.	Strike Furniture, Dressing, SM
		Strike LX & Sound equipment, LX
Mon 19th	09.00 a.m.	Strike Dumbstruck set
	01.00 p.m.	Lunch
	02.00 p.m.	Rig Front of House / continue Strike Set
	04.00 p.m.	Rig on Stage
	06.00 p.m.	Tea
	10.00 p.m.	Call Ends
Tue 20th	09.00 a.m.	Fit-up on Stage
	01.00 p.m.	Lunch
	02.00 p.m.	Continue Fit-up
	06.00 p.m.	Tea
	10.00 p.m.	Call Ends
Wed 21st	09.00 a.m.	LX Focus / Wardrobe Get-in
	01.00 p.m.	Lunch
	02.00 p.m.	Continue Focus
	05.00 p.m.	Tea
	06.00 p.m.	Plot LX
	10.00 p.m.	Call Ends
Thurs 22nd	09.00 a.m.	Plot Sound
	10.30 a.m.	Cast Call for:
	11.00 a.m.	Technical Rehearsal
	01.00 p.m.	Lunch
	02.30 p.m.	Continue Technical
	05.30 p.m.	Tea
	07.00 p.m.	Continue Technical
	10.00 p.m.	Call Ends
Fri 23rd	09.00 a.m.	Set-up to Resume Technical
	09.30 a.m.	Continue Technical
	01.00 p.m.	Lunch
	02.00 p.m.	Technical Work as Required
	05.00 p.m.	Tea
	06.00 p.m.	Dress Rehearsal (with Photographer)
	10.00 p.m.	Call Ends
Sat 24th	09.00 a.m.	Technical Work as Required
	01.00 p.m.	Lunch
	02.00 p.m.	Dress Rehearsal (with Photographer)
	07.10 p.m.	Half Hour Call for:
	07.45 p.m.	First Preview
Mon 26th	09.00 a.m.	Technical Work as Required
	01.00 p.m.	Lunch
	02.00 p.m.	Rehearsal as Called
	07.10 p.m.	Half Hour Call for:
	07.45 p.m.	Second Preview

Production schedule: drama.

ROYAL OPERA HOUSE Wk 40

	Subject to alteration a.m.	Stage Calls p.m.	w/e 27th May, 2006 eve	ORR
SUNDAY 21 R	9.00 hang, set & focus Rake's Progress	2.00-4.00 light Rake 4.00 c/over to Homage 5.00 tech. & focus Homage & light as poss	8.00 strike to clear stage 9.30 finish	ORR 1
MON 22 R	7.30 c/over 11.30-2.30 Bluebeard/ Erwartung + Orch sets, lights, props **9.00-6.00 build Tosca**	2.30 paint bottom of iron	7.30 SLEEPING BEAUTY 10.30 c/over 11.30 finish	Tosca 10.30 Act I 2.30 Act I **ORR2** Bluebeard 3.30 standby
TUES 23 B	7.30 c/over 11.00-2.00 Duke Bluebeard's Castle/ Erwartung general prodn desk in Orch. Stalls Fire Drill **8.30-6.30 build Tosca**	continue tech. to 2.30 [Lift unavailable until 5pm]	7.30 SLEEPING BEAUTY 10.30 c/over 11.30 finish	Tosca 10.30 Act II 2.30 Act II **ORR2** prep Figaro
WED 24 R	8.30 c/over 11.45-2.45 Rake's Progress + pno sets, lights, props **8.30-6.30 build Tosca**	[Lift unavailable until 5pm] **Studio Theatre:** 2.30-5.30 Orch alone: Rake's Progress prog.	7.30 CYRANO 10.30 c/over 11.30 finish	Tosca 10.30 II & III 2.30 III & I **ORR2** Figaro 3.30 Act I
THURS 25 B	7.30 c/over 10.45-2.15 Homage + pno sets, lights, props **9.00-6.00 build Tosca**	3.00-6.00 Orch in Pit alone Rake's Progress Iron down	7.30 SLEEPING BEAUTY 10.30 c/over 11.30 finish	Tosca 10.30 Act I 2.30 Act II **ORR2** Figaro 10.30 Act I 2.30 Act II
FRI 26 R	8.30 c/over [piano delivery via giraffe door] 11.45-2.45 Diverts + pno sets, lights, props **9.00-6.00 build Tosca**	**Studio Theatre:** 3.00-6.00 Orch alone: Tosca	7.30 (1) BLUEBEARD ERWARTUNG 9.45 c/over 11.30 finish	Tosca 10.30 II 2.30 III **ORR2** Figaro 10.30 Act I 2.30 Act I
SAT 27 B	7.30 c/over 11.00-2.30 Rake/ Diverts t.b.c./ Homage [La Valse t.b.c.] + Orch sets, lights, props **9.00-6.00 build Tosca**		7.00 CYRANO (last) 10.00 c/over 11.00 finish o/night call get-out Cyrano	Tosca 10.30 Act I 2.30 **ORR2** Figaro 10.30 Act II

Sunday, 28th May: Tosca technical

Technical Office

Production schedule: opera.

Summary

What is described above is the beginning of an understanding of the process of lighting a production – an overview of the role of the lighting designer. What is not described, however, is what specifically a lighting designer needs to know about the ideas and equipment behind the term 'stage lighting' in order to carry out this role – that is what awaits the reader in the rest of this book.

2 THE TEXT

As we have already discussed in the preceding chapter, not all staged productions start with a written text. The word 'text' in this context can apply equally to a musical score, a novel on which a stage production is to be based or, similarly, a biography, a painting, a film, and so on – really, any original source material. And a good and thorough knowledge and understanding of the 'text' forms a vital part of the lighting designer's job.

Where a play text is the starting point for a production, it is a very important part of the job to become extremely familiar with the *bare bones* of the written word on which the *flesh* of the production will be built.

WORKING WITH A TEXT

In the case of working from a written play text, the lighting designer will get to know the piece thoroughly by reading and re-reading it any number of times – just as when music is involved, the need is similarly to fully immerse oneself in it by listening to it over and over again.

On each new reading or visit to the text, the lighting designer should approach with different ambitions, aiming to glean different things. Typically, for example, the following:

- A basic overview of the piece – what happens and when.
- A more detailed consideration of plot and character – why things happen.
- A careful consideration of where the action is set at any moment – location, season, time of day, etc.
- A realization of the overriding mood or dramatic atmosphere in any scene.

- An interpretation of the through-line of dramatic tension – its highs and lows.

It may be that to do the above, a lighting designer may resort to various 'tricks'; for example:

- imagining the scenes in any setting that comes to mind (ignoring the stage directions);
- imagining a period play into a modern setting (thereby finding what contemporary issues it reminds you of);
- casting the play from amongst your friends, or the famous;
- reading the play through with friends or colleagues;
- giving different colours or shapes to various sections of the play;
- deciding what animal the different characters in the play remind you of.

...any of these may or may not be useful, depending on the individual thought processes of the lighting designer, but all are aimed at finding out what you feel the play is about, how it communicates its ideas and emotions, where its dramatic tensions lie, and what, therefore, you as a designer feel about the piece.

It is very difficult to work on a piece – work that, after all, can be very demanding – if you do not like it. So part of the early part of the process inevitably involves learning to *love* the piece – and where this is not too easy, taking time to find its redeeming characteristics. For this, the director and designer can often be a big help as they, too, must want to work on the production, and their ideas about its strengths can be very usefully adopted.

In reality, whatever one feels about a piece, there has to be some connection with it, if only

Research scrapbooks.

intellectual, in order to be able to design – because designing, with its inherent need to create, is all about interpretation. And one can only interpret something that one understands.

BACKGROUND RESEARCH

Alongside working with the text, the lighting designer may well also read around the subject – and this may include reading other plays by the same author, or other pieces set in the same period or milieu; researching the geographical setting or historical period of the piece; the genre in which it is set; or its place in the fashion or style of the period. References may also be sought in other forms of art – painting or sculpture – or in other theatrically linked pieces, and so on.

During this process the lighting designer should take careful notes so that they can be returned to later – and keep them usefully at hand – often creating a version of the text for this very purpose, or a separate scrapbook or books (*see* illustration above).

It is very important at this point that the lighting designer should remember that the text is not the finished product and, therefore in studying it in so detailed a way, they must take care not to become too attached to any interpretations they may make of it – interpretations that, if they are not careful, may well steer them a long way from where other people see the piece going. So, although this period of study may happen initially in isolation, it is best mixed as soon as possible with discussions involving the other influential members of the creative team, most importantly the director and the designer.

UNDERSTANDING THE TEXT

As has already been stated, it is important that the lighting designer has a clear and thorough understanding of the text. In this it is not so necessary that they have a deeply profound understanding of the piece in terms of its historical or literary merits: what is important is that the lighting designer understands the dramatic message that the text, and later the performance of that text, is attempting to convey at any moment. Admittedly the research into the background of the text may help facilitate this, but it is the dramatic weight of any one moment of the play that the lighting needs to support and enhance, not its place in world literature.

In order to be good at this, the student lighting designer must take every opportunity to see any work they can, and review it for its strengths and merits, viewing all that they see for its potential as a piece to light. Looking at the work of others in the field can also help develop and refine these skills – as well as provide new ideas – after all, in this arena there is no greater compliment to a lighting designer than to have their ideas stolen!

Obviously the lighting designer is also charged with the responsibility to undertake a number of other things, which may include making the scenery and the stage around it fit in terms of location, time of day, season, and so on. Using lighting to communicate such fairly obvious information (not always as easy to achieve as to state) is an important part of the lighting designer's art, and naturally differs in importance with each production.

Summary

An in-depth knowledge of the 'text', whether written or other, cannot but aid the lighting designer in their work. However, as we have seen, it is only part of the process, although one not to be underestimated. What follows in the process – the meetings and discussions – can only really come to fruition if this essential preliminary stage is undertaken seriously and studiously. However, it is important to remember, for example, that a play as a written text is not a play – it is only really a play when it is in performance.

3 THE DIRECTOR AND THE DESIGNER

It is very important that the lighting designer establishes and retains a good working relationship with everyone involved with the production; certainly anything less than this only makes life more difficult than it need be. There is no room in a busy production schedule for ego and insecurity (although unfortunately, human nature being what it is, there is often enough of it about!), and the process works so much better in an atmosphere of trust and respect. This is particularly the case at the apex of the creative team, which is commonly represented by the director and the designer, and (hopefully) the lighting designer. In many productions this trio is the team, more than any other, that originates and develops the overall style of the production.

THE PRODUCTION STYLE

In the case of a play, opera or musical, it is not uncommon for the director and designer (with the musical director and choreographer where applicable) to be the main instigators of the overall production style. To be clear, the 'production style' is the particular interpretation or slant that the piece is to have on any new staging, and it is usually deeply wedded to the way that the director, in particular, interprets the text. Although re-stagings do happen, particularly in classical dance and opera, on most occasions a director's motivation for doing a piece is to make it fresh; to give it a contemporary relevance; and to bring to it new and revealing insights of their own.

Without different production styles and ways of viewing a piece, every *Hamlet*, every *Tosca*, every *Swan Lake* would simply be a carbon copy of an original production, and the art forms they represent would be extremely stale and ultimately moribund. All of this usually means that a new production will look quite different from any

A designer placing scenic elements within his model box.

17

other outing of the same piece – a unique styling will be given to the piece to further display its re-interpretation – the 'production style'. And this is, of course, where the designer, and then the lighting designer, comes in.

THE DESIGNER AND THE DESIGN

The designer's role is more than anything one of interpretation and translation – translating the ideas of the production style and the play on to the stage. Thus they, too, will go through a similarly detailed process of discovering a text, as described in the previous chapter.

The designer has to deal (among other things) with placing on stage a construction that will allow the piece to function effectively and look apposite and good. At two extremes the designer has to worry about the rather mundane – for example, providing the right number and positioning of entrances and exits – and the esoteric: these, and all other parts of the stage, should be totally in tune with the dramatic tone of the production at all times. And to a great extent the *tone* will be dictated by the director's interpretation. Thus the director and designer often work 'hand in glove' to create a total, distinct, often complex, and ultimately immutable production style.

In this case, when the director and designer lead, and even when the lighting designer has been brought in at the very start of the process, the latter is often seen as merely an adviser who waits to be handed down various decisions. The lighting designer may be asked to contribute as ideas progress, but it is understood that until the director/designer team has come up with the interpretation that will dictate the production style, then they are in the wings waiting their turn. Quite often they are not even invited to the beginning of the process, and the first time the lighting designer is brought in, a scale model of the set and full costume drawings have already been created. This is not to say, however, that the lighting designer will not eventually have a chance to make their own artistic or creative contribution, as we shall see.

The lighting designer does not always have to take second place, and this is not the case on occasions when they take the role of the designer, and the lighting is given the status of the most important aspect of the staging, above that of the setting. This can occur for a number of reasons – often, however, it is simply because for one reason or another (often financial) there is to be very little structure on stage, and the lighting has thus become the set! In order to allow full and fluid use of a stage this is often particularly the case in the creating and staging of modern or contemporary dance.

WORKING WITH THE DESIGN

The lighting designer usually has a number of things with which to work that originate with the designer(s). This includes a scale model of the set as it will appear on stage, being usually a 1:25 three-dimensional, fully coloured and textured

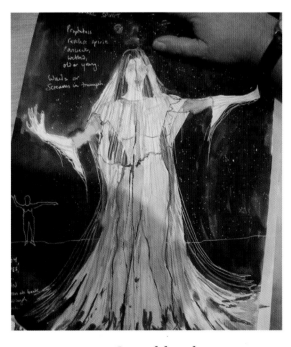

*ABOVE AND OPPOSITE: **Set models and costume drawings are important reference material for the lighting designer.***

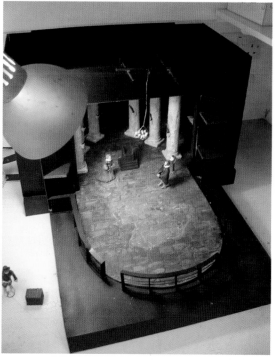

representation of the set, placed in a similarly scaled model of the main aspects of the theatre space. Also often created are detailed and fully coloured costume drawings, often with fabric samples attached.

The lighting designer may also have access to copies of the designer's other research material – visuals in particular – and other items, some possibly coming also from the director, such as videos, historical documentation, and so on.

It is obviously important that the lighting designer should study all this material and incorporate it into their own set of references. In the case of the model, they can also make good use of it by taking time to do the following:

- Take on board and learn thoroughly the colouring and texture of the set – become familiar with it.
- Work through the play and learn how it is likely to be set on the staging provided.
- Try light on the model – using lanterns, torches, whatever is at hand – looking for good and effective angles and ways to address the set and the actors on it: experiment.
- Try different colour washes (possibly also gobo washes) to see how the set changes under coloured (and shaped) light.

- Make use of the model in discussions with director and designer(s) so that you all remain clear about how the production is going to work.

A similar approach is essential when dealing with costume drawings and, eventually, the costumes in preparation. The lighting designer can try lighting the diagrams, the fabric samples and the finished costumes, in particular to see how different coloured light will work on them – coloured light can have very spectacular and often surprising effects (*see* page 30).

THE IMPORTANCE OF COMMUNICATION

Effective and thorough lines of communication between the lighting designer, the director and designer, as well as all the production team, are of course essential. In the case of the director and designer, it is especially important for the lighting designer to communicate with them in an open and productive manner, and for the process to be seen by all concerned as a two-way street, and not just a matter of dictates or instructions. This vital element of the process is discussed in more detail in Chapter 5 (*see* page 37).

Summary

As hopefully has become clear by now, it is essential that the lighting designer understands the originating impulse behind a production, and then is sufficiently informed about it to be able to develop this impulse and the ideas behind it. It is also important that these ideas, particularly in the hands of the director/designer, become the production style that calls the shots for most of what follows, and will make the production a great success (or not!). The lighting designer must therefore do their homework properly before moving on with their work, whether this is technical or artistic. And this homework, by necessity, is informed by a thorough understanding of the theory that lies behind stage lighting.

PREVIOUS PAGE: Two set models and details for Schiller's play Mary Stuart *from designers Lorna Ritchie (bottom) and Chryssanthy Korfidou (top).*

4   THE THEORY

The theory behind stage lighting is very simple, and one aspect of the real work of a lighting designer is to find new ways to use equipment, and continue to investigate the theories behind its use on each occasion. The theory falls into five easily understood categories:

- angle
- shape
- colour
- movement
- composition

It is worth noting that the first three of these categories are descriptive of the light itself, and that all apparent light sources have angle, shape and colour, whereas the last two – movement and composition – are about how we use light, and how we make effective pictures with it.

All these cases, however, are quite simply about how light conveys information to the viewer. This in turn is based on what we, as individuals, already know about the way light works in the world around us – a knowledge that we obtain and build on almost from the very moment of our birth. In other words, the lighting designer is working to an audience that, quite often, without even really being aware of it, is already expert in the use and interpretation of light – and also in particular of how light helps to make pictures and tell stories. It is worth noting at this point that today's audience is also extremely literate in deciphering pictures because of their huge exposure to stage, film and televisual storytelling.

We will return later to the overall way in which light can tell a story, evoke an emotion, or simply convey information; but let us start by examining the essential and most basic principles or components of light itself, as listed previously.

ANGLE

The angle at which a beam of light hits an object can reveal or convey very different things. The two extremes in this, and a good starting point for our discussion, are *clarity* and *interest* (*see* illustrations overleaf [top]).

The dancers in the first picture are very clear, in that we can see them totally; but those in the second picture are much more interesting, full of curiosity and movement, even though some of the detail is far from clear. The dichotomy between these two very possible ambitions for our lighting – clarity and interest – in that both seemingly oppose each other in realization is at the heart of much of the decision-making that a lighting design is faced with – namely which to favour.

As we explore direction of light further we can see that different angles of light give us differing proportions of these two ideas. The illustrations overleaf show the five basic angles of light, namely front, back, side, top and up, and all other angles of light are just variations on these five, even though there are 360 degrees of angles available in 360 degrees of different planes, making (without splitting degrees) 129,600 alternative positions! A few examples of the most common combinations of these five fundamental positions demonstrate how they make up the basis of all other positions (*see* photos on page 23).

In looking at lighting angles we may well need to consider where a light source is supposedly coming from, and the justification can be literal or abstract (that is, the source could be said to be the sun or a table lamp), or it could be non-justified

In front *light these performers are clearly visible, whereas...*

...in back *light they are not so visible; but what a much more interesting and dramatic picture we now have here.*

Different angles in use. Left to right: side light; top light; up light.

(the audience is not expected to see a link between the light source used and any usual light source). Whatever the case, the choice of angle is dependent on what we are trying to convey, so let us also label the illustrations on page 22 in terms of their emotional weight or apparent meaning:

- *Flat light* can be said to be boring, in that if there are no shadows there will equally be no interest. But in a different context (for instance, used powerfully) it also has an interrogatory look.
- *Back light* can be described as spooky or mysterious.
- *Side light* is interesting and powerful, if somewhat abstract.
- *Top light* can also be spooky and mysterious, but it can look oppressive and dominating too – it appears to push down on the object being lit.
- *Up light* is strange, weird and most unusual – it is, after all, the most unlikely of natural light angles.
- *High front light* is a good balance between interesting and clear, and also happens to mimic angles of light we are very used to seeing – a source at that angle could be the sun, a street light, or an interior light.
- *Cross light* is not as normal as high front light, but it is less strange than pure side light as it comes from above.

One of the most important things we can learn from this exploration is that *shadow is as important as light* when it comes to revealing or showing the shape and form of an object. Other important concepts also revealed can be listed thus:

- Flat lighting, where the light seems to originate with the viewer and therefore eradicates shadow, produces a boring, 'flat' picture.
- High angles of light make very dramatic pictures, but are not very good for visibility.
- Average angles that are neither particularly high nor flat, are good for visibility, are usually very believable, but not overly dramatic.
- Lighting angles similar to those of real light sources – for instance, key sources such as the

The combination of top and front gives a high side angle from in front of the object.

The combination of side and top gives a high side light, usually referred to as a 'cross' light. From **Attempts on her Life.** *Lighting by David Bishop.*

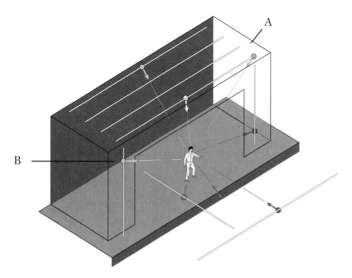

Flat light
Back light
Side light
Top light
Up light
High front light
High side light
High side front light

The basic lighting angles.

Note how the light crossing the rear of the picture, skimming the wall, clearly reveals the brickwork behind the performer.

sun, lamp posts, and so on – help to enhance the reality of a setting.

In addition we can also clearly see that:

- Angles that skim objects are good for showing texture (see illustration [left]).
- Dramatic angles add interest and create mood (*see* illustration [page 25, top]).
- Clear and exciting angles of light add tension, and therefore drama to a stage picture (*see* illustration [page 25, bottom]).

Combining Angles

The five basic angles of light can appear to be very different when used in combination, but remembering what they provide in isolation allows us to identify what they are contributing in any particular picture. (The use of angles to create a general cover of light for a stage area is discussed in full on page 53.) It is also worth noting that the use of too many angles of light simply blurs the picture: as is often the case, *less is more*.

A combination of angles allows us to combine their uses – for instance, an angle for definition combining with an angle for drama (*see* illustration on page 40).

ABOVE: Dramatic lighting angles are highly evocative. From Troilus and Cressida *by New Audience, New York. Lighting by Scott Zielinski.*

RIGHT: Few and clear angles are highly dramatic. From Dance of the Vampires. *Lighting by Ken Billington.*

Back light with high front light, giving clarity and drama.

The objects in the scene with back light are so much clearer (and more interesting) than in the photograph where back light is absent.

Of course, we must remember to separate in our minds the number of lanterns used from the number of sources of light we are creating, as any number of lanterns can be used to create the appearance of a single lighting source, as we shall discover (*see* page 53).

Back Light

What is most notable here is how back light, which in isolation fails the clarity test so thoroughly it can rarely and then only briefly be used on its own, in combination with other angles really becomes a force to be reckoned with – especially as a definer of shape and form (compare the illustration above right with the illustration on page 22 [top left]).

This underlines an important feature of theatre lighting – its ability to project towards the viewer the object being lit. Back light or rim light (light that silhouettes the object) identifies to the viewer

the three-dimensionality of the object – reveals its form – and in doing so appears to push the object towards the viewer, making it clearer. The importance of this concept cannot be stressed enough (see the illustrations above).

Key Light

Another important idea to come from this analysis of lighting angles is that of *key*. This is simply the idea that a stage picture with a strong, dominant source of light is more attractive than one without, not the least reason for this being because a strong key, as from sunlight for example, is something we find naturally appealing and that we recognize. Obviously making one particular source stronger than another is not particularly difficult to achieve, it is just a matter of adjusting levels and, as the illustration opposite shows, does look highly effective.

Hiawatha *for Torch Theatre Company. Lighting design by Neil Fraser.*

Summary: Lighting Angles

We can summarize what we have said about lighting angles, as follows:

- The direction from which a light hits an object, as seen by the audience, is vital when it comes to how that object will look.
- Lighting as defined by its angle of approach can be *flat* or *fascinating*; it can be *realistic* or *strange*; it can be *believable* or *false*.
- Clarity not only comes from the use of front light. Front light may enhance visibility, but light emanating from behind or to the side of an object can also aid clarity.
- The ways in which any of these can be realized is down to the way we see light working in the real world.

- A dominant single light source can be highly effective; such a light source is called a 'key'.

Alongside our knowledge of how individual lighting angles work in different ways, we also can sum up what we have said about lighting angles generally in the following concepts:

- Light reveals form.
- Total visibility is often boring.
- Shadow enhances light.
- Too many sources will mean a loss of definition.
- A dominant key source is highly effective.

A gobo is an etched metal cut-out, or a heat-resistant glass slide that fits inside a profile spotlight or an intelligent unit (see pages 63 and 71) and thus shapes the beam of light coming from this type of unit.

SHAPE

As we have already said, all beams of light have shape, although in the case of a very softly focused light this may not be at all apparent. Similarly, the conventional ellipse created by a circular beam being directed at an angle to a stage may also be so familiar as to pass unnoticed by an audience. This may also be true of a hard edge that is simply being used to cut off spill from the beam – for example, from the side or front of a stage.

However, where the shape of a beam of light has a clear shape, then generally it can be said to have, or to convey, meaning. The shaping of beams of light is made by the use of shutters or gobos (*see* illustration). As this shows, the shape of a light can be straightforward, such as a boxed light to define a room; or very intricate, to create the effect of light coming through a Venetian blind or stained-glass window. Whatever the case, shape can clearly be seen as an important device to define mood or place, if and when we wish to use it.

Summary: Shaped Light Conveys Information

- Shapes in light send the audience messages about mood and location; these can be subtle or not so subtle.
- Hard, visible shapes are either extremely descriptive (as in a window gobo) or aggressive (as in a hard, focused spotlight).
- Soft, invisible shapes are passive and often make no comment.

RIGHT: A single wide-angle beam casts a strong defining shape across a stage.

BELOW RIGHT: Creative use of colour can enhance the simplest picture.

COLOUR

Colour is perhaps the most emotive of aspects of stage lighting. The colours in the world around us, and in the things we choose to wear or to decorate our most intimate living spaces, mean much to us. We talk about loving or hating colours – 'I love the colour of that wallpaper', 'I hate the colour of that tie' – and thus we make distinct choices directly concerned with colour (after all, we do not talk about loving and hating angles of light or particular shapes!); indeed, there are whole industries devoted to the psychology and interpretation of our relationship as humans to colour.

All light is of some colour – there is really no such thing as 'white light' or colourless light – but naturally in many cases the colour is not strictly overt.

In creating a stage picture, colour can be used very simply and literally to convey many

naturalistic things: a sunny day, a sunset, moonlight, a neon sign, a traffic light, a television screen, a black and white movie, the sea, night, a fire, a waterfall, and so on. But in doing all of these, it is also coloured light that will be surrounding these images and giving them a context in which to exist. And this light will be of subtler hues and tints of colour and is thus more commonly used because of this – variations really on the idea of uncoloured or white light.

Many things in light work comparatively – thus a bright light bursting from the darkness of a 'blackout' will have much more impact than the same light being added to an already brightly lit stage. In much the same way, colour in light always appears to our eyes in reference to the colour that surrounds it. It is notable in this that lighting for camera (film, video or television) has to follow a very precise method to apply 'colour' and 'white balancing', as the instruments that record the light are in no way as sophisticated as our eyes. The latter adjust acutely to context in a way that the inventions of man simply cannot cope with – as anyone who has taken photographs using normal film in theatre conditions can testify.

In the abstract, bright or dark colours can be very dramatic and send loud and clear messages to an audience. And strong colours used in isolation do send emotional messages – for example purple for passion, or green for envy. Red alone can read as passion, blood, war, rage, sex or love. The lighter colours also affect the audience, but less obtrusively, and it is with these colours therefore that we can hope to effect the dramatic tension of a piece in a sensitive and discrete manner. These lighter colours (hues and tints) can help us to establish and define a drama by dictating the subtle colour of the basic light we use on stage. We are thus in control of the colour of daylight, sunlight or moonlight as depicted on stage. Naturally in this we are particularly interested in how these colours affect skin tones, as some will enhance them, and some will not.

In this area we describe light as being 'warm' or 'cold', with the former more appropriate for lighter subjects, such as comedies or romances, and the latter for darker subjects, such as tragedies or thrillers. Warm colours are in the straw, pink or gold range, and cold colours in the light blue and grey range. Furthermore, warm colours can therefore be said to be 'happy', and cold colours 'sad'. Neutral colour in light, such that it appears colourless (what may be described as 'white light') is still nevertheless a colour, and can be used to suggest the bland, stark or unreal: *see* illustration examples opposite.

Basic Colour Theory and Colour Mixing

Natural daylight appears to our eyes as being generally without colour, but we know from our basic physics lessons that in fact it is made up of all colours, as most of us get to demonstrate with the use of a prism. This rainbow of colour is further defined as containing three primary and three secondary colours, each set of which when mixed together make up the full composition of white light – *see* illustration overleaf.

The colour we see is made up of the wavelengths of light that reflect to us from an object, for without light there is no colour. If we use coloured light, then we reduce the availability of colours to reflect, and this can mean that the colour of objects can radically alter. This is something we should always bear in mind when we use colour – how it will affect the things we light with it.

All light sources, whether natural or artificial, give off different mixtures of colours and therefore appear as different shades of 'white' – another reason why there is no such definable thing as 'white light'. The various 'colours' of these sources are measured in a manner describing them as having differing 'colour temperatures' (*see* illustration on page 33 [top]).

Coloured light that arrives on any stage is made in the lighting instrument in a variety of ways (*see* page 69). Like natural light sources it, too, can be made up of a mixture of many colours, or it can be made up of a single narrow band. In the latter case this is described as *saturated colour* and acknowledges the fact that no amount of all colour (white light) exists within the wavelengths in use. Obviously saturated colour has a particularly

RIGHT AND BELOW: Strong colours used for strong effect: from The Women of Troy *(top) and* The Tempest *(below).*

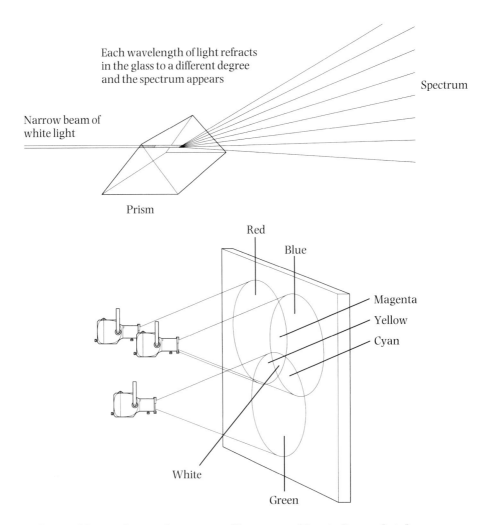

Each wavelength of light refracts
in the glass to a different degree
and the spectrum appears

Spectrum

Narrow beam of
white light

Prism

Red

Blue

Magenta
Yellow
Cyan

White

Green

The seven colours of the rainbow: red, orange, yellow, green, blue, indigo and violet are just convenient labels for various sections of the spectrum. The primary colours in light are green, blue and red; mixed together from three different light sources, they make white. The secondary colours, made by mixing two of the primaries together, are yellow, cyan and magenta, and added together they also make white.

strong effect on what it lights, as it permits the reflection of only a very narrow band of colour (*see* illustration opposite [centre]).

When different lights, using different colours, reach the object they are lighting, they mix together to make a new colour – or, to be more precise, usually what we see is a combination of the new mixed colour, with evidence in the shadows of each lantern of the colours that it derives from. With the lighter colours this poses no real problem, but actually adds to the texturing and interest of the stage picture, going, as it does, generally unnoticed. With stronger colours, however, it can produce some very exciting and extravagant effects, especially when combined with the use of gobos.

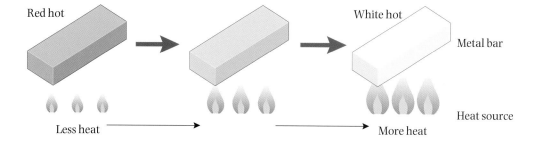

Red hot → White hot

Metal bar

Heat source

Less heat → More heat

ABOVE: Colour temperature is a method of measuring white light sources dependent on their 'colour'; it is measured in degrees Kelvin, and depends on the appearance of the source in question as against a recognized colour scale based on the temperature of a heated metal object.

RIGHT: Manufacturers' swatch books showing the make-up of various colours. Note that the colours as viewed against a white background do not give a true indication of what they will look like in front of light. When choosing colour a lighting designer will hold the gel up and look through it at a light source.

Note: The colours of all swatches have been matched to the originals by scanning and analysing; so all are as accurate as each other, but as the caption above says, maybe not a true indication.

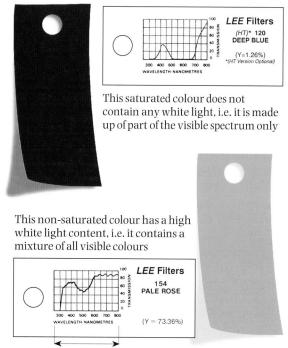

This saturated colour does not contain any white light, i.e. it is made up of part of the visible spectrum only

This non-saturated colour has a high white light content, i.e. it contains a mixture of all visible colours

Range of visible light, i.e. 'white light'

Summary: Colour

We can summarize our thoughts on colour as follows:

- All light has colour.
- Colour is a powerful communicator of emotional mood.
- Colour can be used to help define place, location, time and season.
- In affecting us emotionally, colour is often described in strong terms.
- Lighter colours subtly set a mood.

- Colour (especially lighter colours) are usefully described as being warm or cold.
- Strong colour has great impact.
- Strong colour can easily destroy or overpower a stage picture, and should therefore be used advisedly.
- Colour can mean different things in different contexts, for example red for anger, or red for passion.

MOVEMENT

Movement in light can be of two kinds: actual moving light, as in a flickering fire or reflections in rippling water; and transitional movement, as in the change when one lighting state fades out to another. The former of these is most definitely of lesser significance than the second, and both are best discussed separately.

Moving Light

Moving light can be very alluring – so much so that it can also be rather distracting and should perhaps be used in moderation only. It has its place, as with all stage lighting, in the appropriate setting. For more detail on how to create it, refer to the section 'Special Effects Equipment' on page 71, for it is very much in the realm of special effects that this type of movement belongs.

Smoke and/or mist can be described as very potent additional tools in the lighting designer's arsenal, and they are especially expressive when motion is involved. This is because light, moving or otherwise, is only seen when it is reflected from an object, and so light passing through the air is invisible. However, smoke or mist can be used to reveal light passing through air, and can thus add significantly to the look of stage lighting, and indeed to the very architecture of the stage picture, often making a real contribution to the setting of a piece itself (see illustration on page 73).

Light in Transition

Light in transition forms a very important and potent role in stage lighting, when the appearance, and even more importantly the speed, of the transition can be very telling. The technical details involving the change from one lighting state to another are described in more detail in the section of this book dealing with lighting cues – see page 78. However, generally speaking, fast changes of light are potentially much more dramatic than slow cues. Yet slow (sometimes even unseen) changes of lighting state can be used very subtly to change the mood or the dramatic tempo of the production, and thus influence the observer.

COMPOSITION

The building of lighting states – or of stage pictures – is defined by the creative need of any given moment. These needs can be literal or abstract or anywhere in between. For example, the lighting may need to suggest a hot summer's day – a very literal use of light – or to express the notion of oppression – a quite abstract concept. But things are rarely even this simple, and quite often what is required is a hot summer's day that also suggests oppression!

It is the lighting designer's job (with the guidance of others, and in particular the director and designer) to know how best to achieve this – and this knowledge itself comes from experience, with the use of equipment and the aspects of light we have already discussed, namely angle, shape, colour and movement.

In fact we have already begun building our understanding of composition by starting to make value judgements concerning these aspects of lighting. We have had to decide which angles of light do what, and which are therefore most effective. Similarly with shape, and colour, and movement – at all times we are deciding what we like and what we do not, what works and what does not. In part we have already started to build pictures, and naturally this only continues and becomes more sophisticated as we use all these aspects in combination, and then apply them to our understanding of a given piece of drama.

But how do we decide what is 'right'? For the most part, of course, there is no 'right' and 'wrong', and this important concept affords us the freedom to explore and discover our own truths, and ultimately our own style. However, we cannot be too complacent here, as there is still such a thing as effective or ineffective lighting, and of course we want to provide the first of these within our work, and not the second. So it is important that we take every opportunity to refine and develop our ideas as to what is effective, and this we can do in a number of ways, as follows:

- **Observe** – look at light everywhere and work out how it is being created and how you would recreate it on stage – light in the real world outdoors, indoors, on film, and on stage.

- **Educate** – look at how artists have used light and (even regardless of light) how they have composed their pictures – this applies to painters in particular – good examples being Rembrandt, Caravaggio, Hockney.
- **Practice** – take every opportunity to try out ideas, new things, better things; to explore, and to create with light.

We must also recognize that the facets of light, as described above, also combine with a need to know how much light to use – what quantities of light to put where.

How Much Light?

The amount of light to use from a single unit, or generally for any scene, is, of course, a vital decision that the lighting designer has to make when creating a stage picture. More than anything, he or she must avoid the trap of using too much light; and this is a trap because it seems so appealing, more light seeming to suggest greater clarity – greater impact – greater anything! Whereas often the truth is quite the reverse, as we saw in the illustration top right on page 22. Certainly impact *can* be made with brilliance, but subtle nuance can very often be made with a clever balancing act between light sources – and shadow is all-important in this. Too much light simply denies us shadow.

So it is important that we develop a 'good eye', an appreciation of what makes a good picture, and of how to balance light sources in order to achieve this. We need to see, not just look, and as with many such art forms, practice makes perfect.

CONCLUSION

The theory by which a lighting designer works is derived from a knowledge of what we see in the real world, and how these ideas are best applied on stage. What he or she then needs is an understanding of the means to achieve this, and what is required on each occasion; and this imaginative process is a combination of the technical and the artistic.

Summary: What can Stage Lighting Achieve?

What follows is an attempt at listing what we now know we can strive to achieve, suggest, enhance or create with stage lighting, although not all will necessarily be appropriate on each occasion, of course:

- *Visibility:* it allows us to see the action clearly.
- *Setting:* it helps us identify where we are.
- *Location:* it describes the locale.
- *Time:* it tells us what time of day it is...
- *Season:* ...and tells us when in the year we are.

- *Atmosphere:* it informs us of the dramatic mood of a scene.
- *Highlighting:* it directs our attention.
- *Texturing:* it makes a stage picture alluring and detailed.
- *Stylization:* it pinpoints and creates a style or genre.
- *Awe:* it creates special effects, amazes and enthrals us.

5 MEETINGS AND DISCUSSIONS

The initial stages of working on a production involve many meetings and discussions: group, team and 'one-to-one' meetings with individuals such as the director and designer, the head of the Lighting Department, and so on. One important type of group meeting is the Production Meeting, which often involves the largest get-together of the production team. In fact at some point, one or several 'production meetings' will take place that may well require *all* the team to be present.

Whatever the size, any of these meetings can be quite daunting – although, of course, they are only there to help move things on, provide information, and establish lines of communication.

GOOD RULES FOR MEETINGS

There are several important points that you should remember during the conversations that will occur during the initial meetings:

- Make sure you take time to listen carefully to others.
- Make thorough and clear notes.
- Do not fail to express you own opinions, but do not speak without thinking – you can always come back later. Certainly, do not speak if you have nothing to say!
- Do not promise more than you are reasonably going to be able to deliver, but...
- Do think and talk inspirationally – free thinking can spark many ideas – but only in the right company, and yet...
- Ask as many questions as you like – the correct

atmosphere for these conversations should be that there is no such thing as a 'silly question'.
- Question others' ideas, but always in a positive and supportive manner.
- Avoid confrontation, especially at an early stage.
- Be prepared, but also do not be afraid to seek advice and support from others in the team – it is a sign of maturity, not ignorance, to say, 'I don't know about that, please tell me...'
- In conversations with important team members – the director or designer – it is a good thing to have something to say that displays your understanding of the text (if there is one): so make sure you have done your preparation.

LATER MEETINGS

Directors and designers come in many shapes and sizes! Some want to dictate every move made by every member of the team, and this – to a lighting designer – can mean telling you where to put every instrument, what colours to use, and so on. They have every right to do this, but it can seem to rather negate the purpose of having appointed a well qualified lighting designer! At the other end of the scale some people put in charge of productions seem to think that communication will come about by some form of telepathy and almost seem to shun conversation, giving little or no instructions. Directors and designers are very busy people, but even a few well chosen moments and comments can make all the difference.

It is important that the lighting designer has a very clear understanding of what is being asked of them – and thus so too the lighting. This can come in many ways, seeing rehearsals being a significant one. The lighting designer should certainly

OPPOSITE: Not all meetings should end like this!

not avoid asking questions of their fellow team members directly when necessary, and should do so as soon as possible – at the very least while the answer can still be incorporated within the lighting design.

There is nothing worse than realizing something about the production too late to be able to incorporate it, and so in the later stages of the production process, when things become pressured, it is important to be fully in charge of all elements of the process. Part of this is knowing fully what is expected and what is going on at every part of the production, and this in turn is partly achieved by asking the right questions in the early stages.

Typical Questions

The kind of question that a lighting designer would be expected to ask of the director or designer can involve many aspects of the production. In the initial stages it is good to get a rough idea of the approach being sought; so one might ask:

- What style of production is this going to be? – a lighting cue per scene, or internal scene cues to express dramatic tension and shifts of emphasis, or many cues and spectacular effects?
- Is there anything specifically required of the lighting?
- Do you mind (are *we* going to mind?) seeing the lighting rig above or around the stage, or is it to be fully or partly masked?
- Is there anything in particular you do not want? (Some directors and designers eschew the use of gobos or strong colour, or any apparent colour at all.)
- Is the set model or costume design accurate? Are these the colours we are going to be using?

Naturally, even at this stage, the questions can also be specific to the text and the production generally. But be aware that often at this early stage the director in particular may not have the answers – because things are still in their mind, this is partly what the rehearsal period is there to answer. On the other hand, whilst great tact has to be used in order not to offend, do not be afraid to ask seemingly obvious questions; for example:

- Is the cut-out cardboard curtain going to be solid (as it appears on the model), or will it be fabric?
- Is the painted sky (on the model) being painted or projected – that is, will it be the responsibility of the scenic art department or the lighting department?

Generally the lighting designer should have an inquiring and open mind. Certainly they should try and be 'in the know' about every aspect of the production in case it affects them, and this would include the asking of technical questions such as:

- Is the masking as shown on the model? Or: What will the masking be?
- How will the set be braced? – that is, what, not shown on the model, is likely to be getting in the way of lighting positions or beams?

And this includes questions to the lighting department of the venue or production, such as:

- Is all your equipment, as listed, in good working order? Or: Is any of your equipment so old it is best avoided?
- Is there anything about your venue that I should know about?
- Where are the sound department likely to, or intending to, rig their speakers?

Also, to help learn a new venue, ask questions such as:

- How does your venue work? Or: What lighting positions are usually favoured?
- Can I see your present rig lit? Or: Could we flash through your present rig to see if anything would be useful?

This last question – asking to see how light works in the venue – can help the lighting designer gauge the way the instruments, and the distances from them to the stage, work in the venue (it is not really about inheriting equipment or ideas from the previous designer!). And, whereas all this can be worked out on paper, nothing quite replaces the opportunity to actually see it for real. It is certainly true that using a venue for a second time usually proves more successful, as the first occasion provides the lighting designer with quite a learning curve, and there is always a great temptation to play safe (one that should be moderately fought).

Much the same thing applies to the creative and technical teams, in that their first time of working together always presents the need for everybody to have to learn each other's preferences and general peccadilloes. If nothing else, you also have to learn how the individuals within the team communicate and, often, it is only at the end of the process, as everything hopefully falls into place, that you realize how much better you could have approached the production with this particular group of people. Thus the first time with any new group of people always presents greater stress than when you know the participants already. This is, of course, one of the reasons that a director or designer will choose to work with the same lighting designer again – not just because they like your work, but because they know you can all work well together and the unexpected is less likely to happen.

In the later stages of the initial process – at a point when the lighting designer has ideas and ambitions of their own for the piece – make sure you avoid contentious or distracting answers to questions by choosing carefully how to phrase or lead a question. For example, if you feel that a pair of window gobos will help support an interior scene, do not ask 'Would this room have light from a window?' Rather say, 'I thought the effect of light through windows would be a good idea, what do you think?' And so avoid asking questions that will only come back to haunt you later.

Communication is obviously the key to this – and it is also obvious that this should be done within a positive and generally supportive atmosphere: one that, needless to a say, the lighting designer has to play a part in creating.

Summary

Important and essential information can be learnt and communicated from meetings of various kinds, and it is thus vital that they are utilized to their full potential. In doing so we can also see that the lines of communication between individuals creates not only efficient and effective work, but also the entire atmosphere of the working experience. Getting it right is thus no small thing, and needs as much thought (and practice) as the exercising of the technical, creative and artistic skills of the lighting designer.

Plainly, with all the information garnered from discussion and research, the lighting designer is now ready to start their work in earnest. The research – both background and communicative – may well continue, and the lighting designer may begin to make preliminary sketches of the design; but they are also waiting for the next important moment, and another vital aspect of the research is needed before a lighting designer has all they need to make their finished design. This is a chance to see the piece in rehearsal.

6 REHEARSALS

Every production is different from those that precede it, and the first chance for a lighting designer to get a clear idea about the uniqueness of the production that they are embarking on may well be at the 'read-through'. This is often held on the first day of rehearsals, when the cast meet and read through the script for the first time together. As this is usually done sitting around in a circle, and is basically an aural experience, it gives limited information to a lighting designer as to what the finished product will actually look like. But it is good for an overall impression, and to feel and be recognized by everybody as part of the team.

Later, more complete and staged rehearsals provide a much better chance for the lighting designer to get a 'feeling' for the piece, and are really the first proper indication of how it will actually appear on stage. The lighting designer may visit rehearsals on any number of occasions, and this is important not only to get a flavour of the piece, but to nourish good relations with the director. However, a key moment is when the lighting designer is invited to a 'run', when the whole play is rehearsed from beginning to end without breaks.

Rehearsals are usually not actually held on the stage that will be used for the final production, and therefore the lighting designer has to approach rehearsals with caution. For example, they need to make sure they understand clearly what it is they are about to see – that is, what the rehearsal room represents, rather than what it actually is. This may involve the fact that the room is too small and therefore compromises have been made on where people stand; or that levels that will exist on the real set are represented differently in rehearsal, and so on. Nevertheless an effective rehearsal – especially a whole run of the piece – can provide the lighting designer with essential information concerning the overall tone of the piece, and the specific drama of any and all parts of the production.

In fact, information from a 'run' not only gives specific detail to the lighting designer – for example, where people stand, enter and exit, and so on – but it can also inspire their whole approach, as it can be such a rich and vivid experience seeing the, now well rehearsed, performers play their roles. However, more on this later.

In the busy world of commercial theatre, where time is money, there is an enormous pressure to limit rehearsal time to a minimum, and to get a piece on stage and in front of a paying audience as soon as possible. Therefore the lighting designer is often confronted with two less than ideal circumstances: firstly, that the vital run of the play is going to occur so late that it is likely to happen after the date the theatre wants the drawn lighting design delivered; and secondly, that whenever the 'run' does take place, it is likely to be the only one! In worst case scenarios a director may decide not to do a 'run' at all! So how should the lighting designer deal with these possibilities?

- In the case of there being only one proper 'run-through', this simply places an even greater need for the lighting designer to take thorough and comprehensive notes (*see* overleaf).
- When the run postdates the need to deliver the plan, or when there is likely to be no 'run', then

OPPOSITE: A moment from **On the Razzle** *in technical rehearsal.*

it is up to the lighting designer to make sure they have all the essential information they need in order to draw up a design regardless. And this may mean calling more meetings with the relevant parties – especially with the director and other production colleagues – in order to talk through in detail the play that cannot as yet be seen.

- When a 'run' does turn up, even when 'late', it is useful to attend so as to confirm your design decisions, or to find out, at least, what you are going to be in for once inside the theatre – and of course changes *can* be made, however late: this is, after all, the essence of the production period to some extent.

Note-Taking in Rehearsals

Experience is a great teacher, and each individual will have their own methods for note-taking. However, it is useful to remind ourselves of what can be gained from a 'run', and to look at a number of ways of recording this information.

Seeing a 'run' affords the lighting designer the opportunity to see the piece on a human scale – after all, most other information concerning the piece is either in the form of written text, lists, scale drawings, costume sketches or scaled models. A run can certainly tell us any of the following technically useful pieces of information:

- How the set interacts with the action (even if no set is present, some of this should be evident) and thus...
- ...where people are for particular parts of the action, and how they move; and as part of this...
- ...where people enter from, and exit to.
- How the action is presented to the audience – that is, what the audience sees: for example, whether an actor plays a scene facing the audience, or looking to one side, and so on.

But possibly more significantly than this technical information, a 'run' is also a marvellous chance for the lighting designer to understand the emotional weight of any given moment of the production, and to see how these moments add together to give the dramatic momentum to the piece as a whole. It is after all these moments and this dramatic through-line that the lighting designer will be attempting to support and supplement – much as a musical score runs through a film.

Combining these two types of information will give us a sense also of how best to use the equipment we know to be available, or that we know can be hired. So alongside the basic concept of who's where can be entered other ideas, such as which instruments to use, what angles, what colour, and what shape.

It is important to take good notes throughout the production process, and the notion that 'I'll remember that' should never prevail because too much is going on, and even the most vital information can slip your mind. This is especially true in the hustle and newness of a 'run' – particularly if it turns out to be the only one you can see – and especially because, as we have seen, there are many layers of information that can be taken:

- physical: who's where
- technical: what instrument
- emotional: the dramatic temperature

It is therefore probably a good idea to provide as much support for your note-taking as possible, so you should make sure you can watch the 'run' as much as possible, rather than having your head down in your notebook. With this in mind, a number of 'tricks of the trade' are worth mentioning:

- Develop a shorthand: indicate each character with a single letter, a symbol or a number: CS = centre stage, use arrows to indicate movements (*see* page 43). Likewise use symbols to stress important aspects of the piece.
- Have the script and ground plan available, even take the model box to the rehearsal if you think it will be useful to have it next to you as you watch. You may find it a good idea to write your notes alongside the text.
- Provide yourself with a simple way to keep drawing the things that you know will need to be repeatedly drawn – for example, develop a simple sketch to represent the set. Or better still...

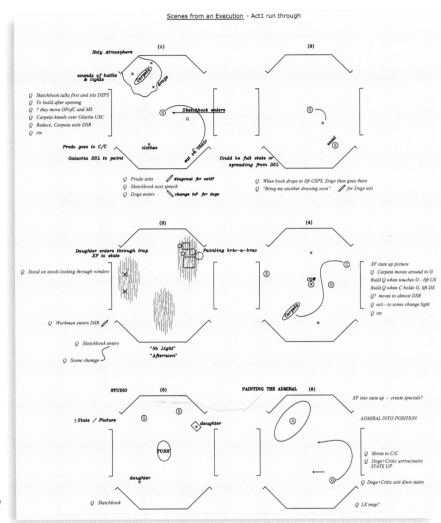

Typically annotated notes.

- ...reduce the ground plan to a very small version, copy this many times, and paste it into your notebook for easy use during the run (the DSM will often have already done this for their masterscript, so borrow theirs) (*see* illustration above).

We noted at the beginning of this section that everyone probably needs to develop their own methods of notation, and this section has only really tried to remind you of how many things there are that need to be borne in mind.

Summary

The rehearsal period can be a vital time for the lighting designer, not only for much needed contemplation of all the technical requirements of the play, but also as a period to find the inspirational and creative needs of the piece.

7 CREATIVITY AND INSPIRATION

Light on stage has been defined as 'an essential and amazingly creative material used to enhance most stage productions'; or as 'a positive and beautiful stage device used to illuminate, create mood, and add drama to the action of a play'. In their seminal books on lighting design, Francis Reid and Richard Pilbrow describe stage lighting respectively as 'a fluid, selective atmospheric dimensional illumination appropriate to the style of a particular production' (*The Stage Lighting Handbook* by Francis Reid, published A&C Black), and as a 'visual design in space and in time' (*Stage Lighting* by Richard Pilbrow, published Nick Hern Books).

In a previous era, Adolphe Appia (1862–1928), the famed Swiss forerunner of modern theatre practice, especially in terms of stage design, discussed 'light revealing form'. His contemporary, Englishman Edward Gordon Craig (1872–1966), discussed the importance of light in 'creating a space (on stage) which harmonises with the thoughts of the poet'.

Charged with these illustrious conceits, it is obvious that as lighting designers we must seek to rise above the more menial aspects of the role, aspiring to be a part of the actual art of the performance. Naturally the menial or basic aspects of the role can dominate a job, and at times seem almost all that we are called upon to provide; however, at other times, and perhaps at some level at all times, we have the opportunity to seek the highest in our art form. For lighting can enable a stage picture to be as one with the greatest art forms – painting, sculpture, music – and help elevate drama into a sublime art form of its own.

OPPOSITE: The Spanish National Dance Company's production Cero sobre cero. *Lighting by Nicholas Fischtel.*

In order to do this we must, as lighting designers, strive to look to our work with the eye of an artist. Look to how our sense of composition and its fine tuning comes from a delicate balance of light-revealing form; provides colour to suggest emotion; and exhibits shape that communicates intent. In all, it is a light that enhances a drama that can in itself tell us something about our very existence – about our very reason for being on this planet. A tall order perhaps, but one that if embraced properly allows us a real chance to fully stretch ourselves, and our art form, both technically and creatively.

THE ART OF PERFORMANCE

In order to feed the idea of stage lighting being an 'art form' in its own right we must educate ourselves in the art of the visual, not only within our own art form but within all others' art so that vital connections can be made: from art form to art form, and from art to life. This does not, of course, mean only the visual arts, because drama is also closely allied to the literary arts – it is not by coincidence that this book starts with the notion of a 'text'.

A designer, in whatever field, must immerse themselves in the form and substance of their art; therefore a lighting designer can never know too much, either about light and how it works, or about theatre itself. It is important to study (and enjoy) all allied fields of entertainment as well as art and literature. What follows are examples of this in action.

INFLUENCES AND SOURCES OF INSPIRATION

Life

The need in the human psyche for drama – for the acting out of stories or situations – is said by historians and psychologists to come from a natural innate human desire to mimic. It follows that it also comes from a similarly in-built need to look at others, and to try and understand their comings and goings. It is a small step, therefore, from *looking* to *contextualizing*, and thence to re-staging events to better understand them, and to show things we know to be true to others.

Thus drama as we know it in the Western Hemisphere derives from the ancient staging of the mythologies of Ancient Greece, and then (after what is usually referred to, aptly enough, as the Dark Ages) is re-invented again in medieval times to tell the stories of the bible.

Whilst theatre history need not trouble us too much here, the historical context of any piece is an important aspect of the research that a lighting designer can do to inform their choices, and improve their level of communication within the production team. However, what is important here is the understanding that observation of real

Light in the world around us can inform and inspire.

events is as vital to understanding lighting as it is to the essence of drama itself.

The observation of light in all aspects of our daily experience is a vital method that a lighting designer can use to keep their own technical realizations within the artificial environment of a theatre connected to what all the audience they serve knows without thinking – namely, what light does in the real world. A lighting designer should therefore make an active and deliberate practice of looking at light at work in the world around them – real and artificial, internal, external, night and day, in all climates, in all parts of the world, and in autumn, spring, summer and winter.

In doing this, it is worth noting that a lighting designer does well to pay particular attention to referencing the following:

- **The unusual or rare:** To take special note of things that one does not get a chance to see often – examples might include holiday locations, such as a Venetian sunset or African moonlight, odd locations, such as inside a cave or an ice house, a swimming pool or a solarium, and so on.
- **The typical or often used:** It is, however, also important to keep refreshing one's memory of more normal things, such as everyday sunlight, moonlight, a forest glade, a shopping mall, especially as many of these can exist in many and endless variations. Certainly one should never become blasé about the everyday aspects and appearance of light.
- **The spectacular or dramatic:** It is naturally always worth noting the exciting or the unusual when it can provide inspiration for similar moments on stage. Shafts of sunlight through trees, clouds or buildings; breathtaking sunsets; or dazzling reflection of light on water, are all worth logging in the mind or, if possible, photographically.
- **Light on people:** Stage light is more often than not about lighting the focal point of our dramatic attention, and for the most part this centres on the performer. Therefore noticing and registering ways that people are lit in the real world, by natural or artificial means, is also vitally important.

Literature

Many plays start as words on the page given to us by the playwright, therefore a familiarity with the written word, especially in an artistic context, cannot be a bad thing. Lighting designers can therefore afford to look to the written word for two kinds of inspiration, namely the indirect and the direct.

Indirect inspiration: This occurs when a lighting designer takes time to become familiar with the way words are used in a literary context, and therefore develops and expands their ability to interpret a text – a skill that can only be enhanced by the lighting designer being 'well read'.

Direct inspiration: This can come from descriptions of light in the form of the written word, within a play text or its stage directions, or in any form of literature. Here are just a few examples:

Summer, from the works of poet John Clare:

I marked the various colours in flat, spreading fields, checkered into closes of different-tinctured grain like the colours of a map; the copper-tinted clover in blossom; the sun tanned green of the ripening hay; the lighter hues of wheat and barley intermixed with the sunny glare of the yellow charlock and the sunset imitation of the scarlet headaches; the blue cornbottles crowding their splendid colours in large sheets over the land and troubling the cornfields with destroying beauty; the different greens of the woodland trees, the dark oak, the paler ash, the mellow lime, the white poplars peeping above the rest like leafy steeples, the grey willow shining chilly in the meadow lake with its flags and long purples crowding the water's edge. I listened with delight to hear the wind whisper among the feather topt reeds, to see the taper bulrush nodding in the gentle curves to the rippling water; and I watched with delight on haymaking evenings the setting sun drop behind the Brigs and peep again through the half-circle of the arches as if he longed to stay.

(From *A Book of Love*, chosen and arranged by John Hadfield, published by Hamish Hamilton, London, 1978.)

From *The Shipping News* by Annie Proulx:

A few torn pieces of early morning cloud the shape and color of salmon fillets. The tender greenish sky hardening as they drove between high snowbanks. A rim of light flooded up, drenched the car. Quoyle's yellow hands with bronze hairs, holding the wheel, Wavey's maroon serge suit like a cloth of gold. Then it was ordinary daylight, the black and white landscape of ice, snow, rock and sky.

(Published by Fourth Estate, London 1993.)

From *Astonishing Splashes of Colour* by Clare Morrall:

Emily and Rose live in a pink house. A house made for winter, with drawn curtains and chairs pulled up close to the gas log-fire. Everything in the house is pleasant and new. It smells new, as if Adrian wants to cancel out the years growing up in our old, second-hand home. There is a heather-pink carpet in the lounge, smooth and restful, and the curtains swirl with shades of pink. They have modern lighting, spotlights behind cheese plants, shaded lights in alcoves, uplights that cast pale ovals on the ceiling. I turn all the lights on when I am there in the evening, but it's not enough. There's a dinginess in this soft lighting that troubles me.

(Published by Tindal Street Press, 2003. The title of Morrall's novel, as she acknowledges, is itself a quote. It comes from J.M. Barrie's '*Peter Pan*': 'For the Neverland is always more or less an island, with astonishing splashes of colour here and there'.)

ART

In art the visual speaks directly to us, and many of the works of great masters are used time and again as reference points by designers and directors alike. Favourites include Rembrandt, Caravaggio, Turner, Hockney, Picasso and many more. Seeking out the works of these painters and becoming familiar with their choice of colour, shape, direction and placement of light within a frame, can greatly aid our own attempts at creating 'pictures' on stage.

Indeed, there exists a term that we can well do with knowing, one that specifically deals with the dynamic way in which many, if not all, of these artists deal with light: it is 'chiaroscuro', deriving from Renaissance Italy and the Italian words for light and dark. And that is what it is about: the interplay between light and dark. Chiaroscuro is important to us in two ways: firstly, it is important to know that this is a significant area of concern for the artist; and secondly, it is an important idea and word for us to use as lighting designers.

Visual art that concerns itself with displaying and organizing the appearance of light is thus a vital source of instruction for the lighting designer, and as such should be used as a resource, both to educate and to inspire.

OTHER MEDIA

Great ideas are always worth knowing, or perhaps even (ultimately) stealing. As the old adage says, 'imitation is the ultimate flattery'. Good lighting can be found in life and in art, but it can also be copied in look, and also in technicality, more easily and closer to home, from photography, television, film and theatre itself. The lighting designer should keep their eye open for inspirational use of light in all these areas, with a view to using whatever appeals when it seems appropriate.

Examples of this would include the brilliant theatrical lighting of Jules Fisher and Peggy Eisenhauer as exhibited in the movie version of *Chicago*, and the brilliant use of light and colour in the films of directors such as Jean-Jacques Beineix (*Betty Blue*, *The Moon in the Gutter*), Bernardo Bertolucci (*The Last Emperor*), Tim Burton (*The Nightmare before Christmas*, *Edward Scissorhands*), Peter Greenaway (*The Cook, the Thief, His Wife and Her Lover*) and Krzysztof Kieslowski with his *Three Colours Trilogy* (*Blue*, *White* and *Red*).

In addition, the work of great cinematographers is naturally also worthwhile viewing: such practitioners as Jack Cardiff, whose use of colour and shade shines out in *The Red Shoes* and *Black Narcissus*; Russell Metty, whose masterpiece is Orson Welles' film noir *Touch of Evil* with its evocative use of darkness struck through with raw light; and Sven Nykvist, who pioneered the use of natural light in such films as *Fanny and Alexander* and *Cries and Whispers* for Ingmar Bergman.

In theatre, the work of contemporary lighting designers is also worth becoming familiar with – designers such as Rick Fisher, Paul Pyant, Andrew Bridge, Peter Mumford, Jennifer Tipton and David Hersey. Indeed, any work of the top lighting designers in the world is, of course, also likely to feed our imaginations, add to our ideas, and broaden our options.

Beautiful side light evokes the world of the 'Grand Master', here in Paul Pyant's work for Women at a Game of Poem Cards.

Summary

The art of lighting design is concerned with an ever-inquiring mind and eye. The discovery of exciting possibilities in light, and the exploration of how to achieve them on stage, is a never-ending journey.

Inspiration can come from within or without, from real life or the fictional setting of entertainment media. Wherever it does come from, one thing is certain: the idea, having been fully understood, has then to be re-communicated by the lighting designer on to their own stage. To do this takes the ability to see clearly what light is doing in the setting they like, and the technical knowledge of how to recreate it elsewhere. Our quest therefore now has to turn to the task of lighting design and the technicalities it involves.

8 THE TASK OF LIGHTING IN PREPARATION

At some stage all the talking, all the planning, all the looking for inspiration and all the thinking about creativity has to stop, and the actual physical graft must take over for a while. This first section on 'the task' is about how that process begins – the creation of a lighting design on paper that sees thoughts turn into action, so that they can in turn become a reality, in which creativity finally becomes light.

USING THE RESEARCH

From the many meetings that the lighting designer has attended, not least with the director and the designer, and having undertaken detailed research, the following information should now have become clear:

- The nature of the production, its overall themes, its *raison d'être*, and its *modus operandi* – meaning its **production style**.
- The director's overall concept for the lighting of the piece, including specific lighting requests.
- The designer's requirements from the lighting.
- The shape, size, appearance and position of the set on stage, and all its various elements.
- The look, colour and use of all the costumes and props.

Lighting design student at work in a RADA design studio.

A Lie of the Mind – Preliminary LX Notes from Script

o Moon wash	sc(i)	I's bedroom during day
o Moon gobo/FX		I's bedroom at night
o Green Moon		Bright morning – B's parents house (winter)
o 2 x Telephone specials	sc(ii)	M couch special night
o Hospital room specials		Armchair special night
o Bed special	sc(iii)	Pars on set
o Hospital screen special		Mobil sign – ropelight/fairies?
o Light under bed?	sc(vi)	Sky panel
o Blue lights in hospital?		Hoarding lights
o B's bed special		Hoarding fluorescents/ architecturals
		Fridge
o Hotel table lamp		Altar
o Soft ceiling light – location/set	sc(vii)	Car headlamps
o Room lights		Light through hotel room door
o Couch special		Suitcase specials
o Room lamp special		Clark Gabel specials
		Hoarding frame #1 Position
o Spiral staircase ropelights		Hoarding frame #2 Position

A lighting designer's list.

- The layout of the theatre, its lighting equipment, its potential rigging positions and all other relevant technical information.
- Other available equipment and/or the **budget** available to hire or buy more.
- The time available for each aspect of the production, and how it is to be arranged: the **production schedule**.
- The personnel available to assist, arrange, install and operate the lighting.
- Any other extraneous limiting factors, for example the requirements of the theatre that limit the positioning of equipment.
- Health and safety issues, and their impact on the creation of the lighting – for example, restrictions on the placing of equipment.

In addition, the essential visit to rehearsals to see a 'run' of the entire play will have elicited more vital information about the tempo, composition and dramatic weight of every moment of the production. And this being the case, the lighting designer should now be in a position to make all the necessary decisions about what the lighting for this production is going to attempt – what it is going to do.

At this point different lighting designers have different techniques in order to achieve what they now need to do, which is to put on to paper their thoughts for the design – that is, draw the design. Some go straight to paper or screen (computer-aided design – CAD – is now often used), and spend a long period at the drawing board or VDU filtering options and making decisions as they draw. Others take time to make these decisions before drawing, so that the drawing process itself becomes merely a final realization of their ideas, and can even be handed over to an assistant.

To be in the situation whereby the drawing of the lighting plan is a mere formality, a lighting designer has to work through all the options, and the following is one way of doing so: first, they read through all their notes, which may include returning to the text once more, with the aim of distilling all necessary information. This information is then listed, and the list put into priority order. Working with this list, the lighting designer then allocates equipment (including the colour, gobos, barn doors and any other necessary items for this equipment), and then beside this they give the position in the theatre for this equipment (*see* illustration above).

A lighting designer's cue synopsis – altered after a lighting session.

Alongside this realization of the drawn design, the lighting designer may also develop and provide a **cue synopsis**. This acts as an *aide memoir* for their own use, and also as a means to communicate the intention of the lighting to the director and any other interested parties. It should, of course, only serve to confirm and embellish for the director (for example) what has already been discussed.

A BASIC STAGE LIGHTING DESIGN

But how do the ideas of lighting theory as described in Chapter 4 combine with the lighting designer's ideas for what they want to provide – to create the lighting of a particular production on stage? In order to bring these two aspects of the work together as a drawn lighting design we must also know how the theory is actually brought to life on stage. And to do this we can do no better than take as our starting point the ideas that go to make a general cover of light for the stage, as this is probably the most fundamental aspect of creating a stage picture: knowing how to cover the stage in even the most basic of ways.

Addressing the Stage

A basic stage is usually too big for any single lighting unit to be able to light it effectively, except in the manner that a football pitch is lit, namely with floodlights – and nobody comes away from a floodlit football match saying, 'My goodness, the lighting was good tonight!'

Why is this so? Because floodlighting only answers the most basic of requirements, namely that we see what is happening. It does not add character or texture, nor does it serve the needs of dramatic development. Yes, we can light a stage with floodlights, or any lantern sufficiently wide-beamed enough to cover the area, and we occasionally do just this when adding colour washes (*see* page 58). Generally, however, not only do we want a look that is superior to that of floodlighting, but we also want greater control of the space. One single light that is either on, or off, does not give us this.

Thus it is important to divide the stage into areas to be lit well, and the size and shape of these areas depends on three main things:

1. The shape and size of the set.
2. The equipment available to light them.
3. The way the stage is going to be used.

In general terms the size of the areas cannot be too big, as we return to the floodlit arena – but neither can they be too small, as equipment will run out and the rig will be over-fussy.

What dividing the stage does allow us to do is make sure that the entire stage is evenly and effectively covered with light. This is often described as a **general cover**, and it is called this because it covers all the stage 'generally', meaning that nothing is missed out, and because it is often *used* generally – it is on hand whenever there is a need for basic or 'general' light at any point on the stage. This does not mean that the 'general cover' need be boring – although a somewhat bland 'general cover' is easy to use over and over again, precisely because it does not impose dramatic ideas. The particular circumstances of any production will dictate the balance here – and it is not unusual for the lighting designer to provide more than one general cover for a production. These 'covers' may come from distinctly different directions and be used singly or in combination.

GENERAL COVER

A standard general cover uses lighting angles that are effective, but not necessarily dramatic. Some lighting designers will avoid using such a basic tool, but nevertheless it is something that has to be learnt, as it forms the basis from which we (and they) deviate.

The usual starting angle for such a 'general' cover is around 45°, both in the horizontal and the vertical (*see* illustration (a) overleaf); this provides an angle that is neither too steep nor too flat, 45° being obviously exactly half way between the vertical and the horizontal – that is, half of 90°. It thus provides a light on a performer that (viewed from the audience before them) flatters the face by appearing as a naturalistic angle and illuminating well – and it does so without being overly dramatically prescriptive. Two such angles opposing each other therefore light a face completely (*see* illustration (b) overleaf).

We then add to this a backlight (or something similar – a side- or cross-light for example) in order to pick the actor out from the set and project them to the audience (*see* page 26, and illustration (c) overleaf). Then we repeat this format over the entire stage space with overlapping areas, giving us a perfectly standard general cover (*see* illustration (d) overleaf).

Creating this cover – planning, focusing and plotting it – is not as easy as it sounds, because to create a smooth and comprehensive general cover successfully is one of the hardest things to achieve in theatre lighting. This is especially true if it is to be exposed for long periods during a production – that is, in the kind of piece where visibility is most important, and the cover will be required to undertake most of the lighting.

To achieve a good 'general cover', the lighting designer is required to make sure the separate areas of light coming from the individual units overlap by precisely the right amount, because too much or too little will create hot spots or dark patches (the bane of every lighting designer's life). Achieving this is often hampered by the equipment not all producing equal amounts of light, or the lights working the same as each other, even when

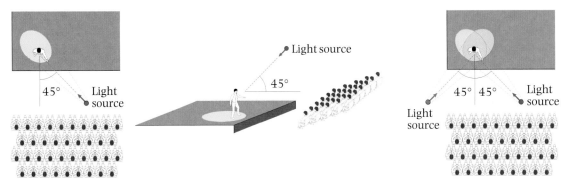

(a) The usual starting angle for such a 'general' cover is around 45°, both in the horizontal and the vertical.

(b) Two such angles opposing each other therefore light a face completely.

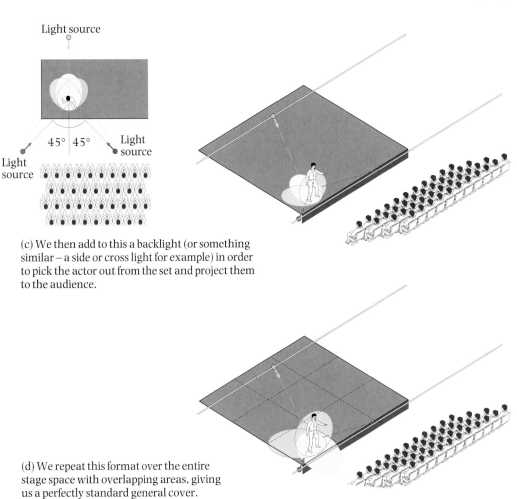

(c) We then add to this a backlight (or something similar – a side or cross light for example) in order to pick the actor out from the set and project them to the audience.

(d) We repeat this format over the entire stage space with overlapping areas, giving us a perfectly standard general cover.

General cover.

the same units are chosen – a usual essential for any one aspect of a cover.

In addition – and obviously – in most cases the stage is not usually bare, and thus objects get in the way, requiring that the areas of the cover be different sizes and not symmetrically arranged. This complexity also adds to the difficulty of making a smooth or seamless general cover that gives the impression of being one entity: often this is the definition or aim of such a cover, that however many units go into its making, it nevertheless gives the impression of being from a single source, as when creating sunlight or moonlight on stage, for example.

General Cover and Key Light

As we discussed in Chapter 4, creating a stage picture with a single dominant source is often to be desired, such a source being called a 'key' (*see* page 26). When this involves a general cover, the means to make one particular direction of light act as a key is quite simple – it is plotted as the brightest source, with the understanding that the other sources, plotted at lower levels, are only there to provide 'fill' – that is, to fill in the picture. Another way to help create a key, or to help one be achieved in the plotting of levels, is simply to use the more

powerful units to provide the light from the key direction.

In the case of sunlight as key, the concept here is that we are replicating the fact that the earth's atmosphere diffuses sunlight and stops it from being a purely singular direction of light, also that local landscape or buildings can in addition provide baffles to redirect the light. On stage, therefore, the 'key' stands in for the direct sunlight, and the 'fill' the diffusion or bounce from atmosphere or other local features.

OTHER COVERS

The use of 'general cover' is described in the case studies that make up the end of this book (pages 100 and 118), but to emphasize the point that a 'general cover' does not always have to follow the rules centred around 45° above, see the plan in the illustration in which side light is used to cover the stage and thus provide the dominant light source, with very few, if any, units rigged front-of-house (FOH) for general light.

Thus a cover can be made from any combination of lighting angles and colours. It can also be made up of gobos, allowing the lighting designer to add *continued on page 58*

RIGHT AND OVERLEAF: **The America Play** *– John Gielgud Theatre RADA. A general cover made up almost entirely of side light. Lighting by Neil Fraser. The plan is viewed side on, with the stage on the left within the dotted circle, and the audience on the right, facing towards the left.*

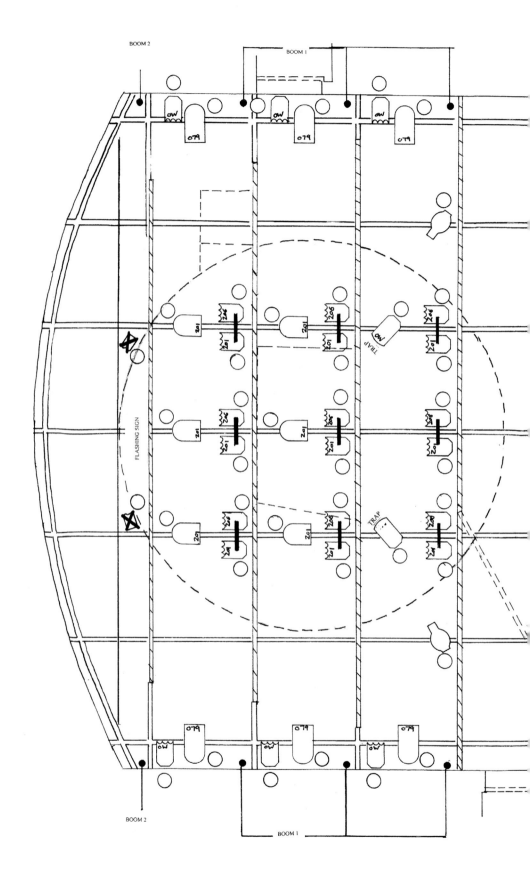

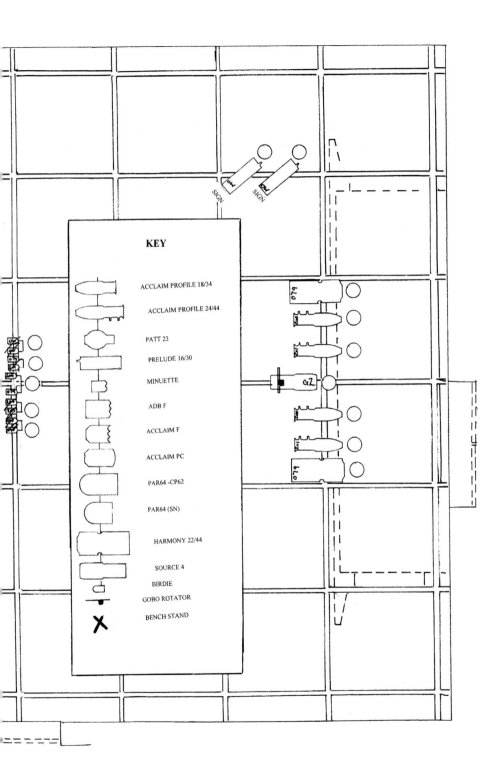

KEY

ACCLAIM PROFILE 18/34

ACCLAIM PROFILE 24/44

PATT 23

PRELUDE 16/30

MINUETTE

ADB F

ACCLAIM F

ACCLAIM PC

PAR64 -CP62

PAR64 (SN)

HARMONY 22/44

SOURCE 4

BIRDIE

GOBO ROTATOR

BENCH STAND

an array of wonderful pattinated light sources to the stage. To do just this the gobo manufacturers provide a wide range of general 'breaks-ups'; these would usually be focused softly within the units to provide the required textured 'general cover' (*see* page 28).

Washes

A wash can be defined as a lighting instrument (or instruments) that adds a very basic wash of light to the stage picture, and in doing so (and in order to be economic with limited equipment or channels of dimming) does not have to adhere to the more precise rules of a 'general cover'. It can therefore often be provided by a very few powerful units – large fresnels, parcans, or even floods (*see* page 68). As such it can be a rather unflattering source of illumination, and is therefore best used in addition to a more precise use of light, such that the wash adds colour or texture whilst other units add precision and edge.

A 'wash' is therefore most often used to add colour to a stage picture (or maybe just the set or backdrop), or to add a kind of texture, as in a 'gobo wash'. In many ways the lighting of a cyclorama is a specific kind of use of a wash of light, and for this, specific floodlights are used (*see* page 67).

Specials

A 'special' is any instrument or instruments used to add a specific and particular feature to the stage lighting, often on a particular person or feature of the set – that is, usually on quite a small area. For example, an actor delivering a monologue or a particularly intense bit of dialogue could be picked out by a 'special', and this may be provided by one or more units. In addition, the choice may be to darken everything around a performer, or simply to dip the surrounding 'cover', or just to add the special and leave all else alone – all according to the preference of the creative team and the degree of subtlety required. Naturally the timing of the change or addition will also add to the degree of subtlety (*see* page 82).

By their very nature, 'specials' are extremely common in stage lighting, and alongside the 'general cover', provide the backbone of many a production. As such, several examples of them are to be found in our case studies (*see* pages 101 and 119). (The term 'special' should not be confused with the term 'special effects'.)

Special Effects

The definition of a special effect is a lighting effect or piece of equipment that offers something other than illumination – for example a water ripple, a mirror ball, or a strobe. As these examples show, a special effect is often unusual and therefore a rarer event on stage, and is often associated with movement of some kind.

See 'Movement' in light on page 34 and 'Special Effects Equipment' on page 71.

DRAWING THE DESIGN: COMMUNICATION AND PAPERWORK

It is, of course, very important that the technical details that make up the artistic ideas of a lighting plan are not lost in translation as they are communicated to the technical team, or indeed the creative team. 'Clarity' and 'detail' are the key words here.

Below are some of the additional pieces of information that a lighting designer may find useful to have at hand when drawing up the design.

Typical Paperwork

Equipment list
What is available, with limited technical information (for instance wattage) – the lighting designer would need to do further research on some of the equipment if they were not familiar with it in order to know what best to use it for – for example beam angles, light output. It is also a good idea to use this list to create a checklist whereby the lighting designer can keep a check on the amount of each unit type they are using, as a mistake here can be very embarrassing.

Circuit field
A handy tool to avoid duplication; the lighting designer crosses off each number as it is allocated to equipment. More often than not this job is taken

by the production's electrician; however, it is still important that the lighting designer does not attempt to use more dimming ways than the venue actually has, so this device is useful simply to keep track of this.

Patch system
What piece of equipment is plugged in where, and how this connects with the dimmers. Often no patch system exists, and socket 1 in the theatre is connected to dimmer 1, but in other cases a more flexible system allows greater choice. Again this may be carried out by the house electricians, but the lighting designer may also want to have their say.

Cue synopsis
A list of lighting cues to be plotted (described on page 52).

Colour call
The cutting list, or what colour goes in what lantern. Once again a piece of paper more useful to the rigging team than to the lighting designer, although the latter may generate it, especially if they are using a CAD programme.

Focus plot
A list of intention, stating what each lantern is designed to do. Or a description of what each unit has been focused to do – that is, compiled after the event in order to have a record in case units are knocked or need replacing.

Hook-up
A US term, and method of providing written information about equipment use – allocation, focus, colour, circuit, and so on (*see* pages 93 and 157).

Cue sheet
A list of the lighting cues that have been plotted – the technical information to go alongside the cue synopsis; for example what cue number, what timing, and so on.

Notebook
A vital piece of equipment – write everything down! It may contain the other most vital piece of information that the lighting designer may need when drawing up the design:

A list of what is required
This list, and the process to develop it, is described more fully on page 51: it will contain such elements as what equipment is being considered for what effect, what colour and other elements are being used in combination with the equipment, and where the equipment will be placed. Certainly this list, alongside the other useful information, should allow the lighting designer to be able to progress with their drawing.

DRAWING THE DESIGN

A lighting designer does not require brilliant drawing skills, although naturally this would do no harm – and in any case, practice makes perfect. Generally a ruler and professional lantern stencils are almost all that is needed, and they are not hard to use; alternatively one of the highly effective computer-aided drawing (CAD) packages, especially aimed at lighting designers, makes for wonderfully professional drawings (*see* illustration overleaf).

What is important is that the drawing successfully communicates to the lighting team what is needed, especially as the lighting designer may be elsewhere at times when it is being used – that is, when technical information is being taken from it, such as during the rigging session.

So, for example, symbols and the placing of them should be clear, with attached localized written notes if needed. And these notes should also include any that will help prompt the lighting designer when they use the plan later as an *aide memoir* for focusing (*see* page 75). Numbering should be large enough for the plan to be reduced and yet remain clear; reductions are often made, especially when the plan is rather unwieldy at the usual 1:25 scale. The lighting designer will also usually include a key on the plan so that the instruments can be clearly identified, and a list of any particular general notes (*see* plan on page 57).

The placing of instruments on a plan follows a usual pattern, as shown in the illustration overleaf,

A paper-free process with a 3D CAD drawing of the effect of a given lighting state (foreground) in use in the Royal Opera House, London.

including information on instrument, colour, gobo, circuiting, and so on.

In drawing up the lighting design the lighting designer will usually start by putting vital information concerning the set on to a new, clean skin of tracing or cartridge paper. This will usually include the basic dimensions of the theatre, and a basic outline of the features of the set, traced through from the designer's ground plan. This drawn plan is then usually placed on top of a plan showing the lighting rigging positions, and

then the lighting designer will begin to place equipment. Unless supremely confident, this plan is drawn in pencil (to allow for corrections) until complete and then, when satisfied, inked over. Naturally if the pencilled plan has become overly messy, a new skin can easily be placed over it for the inking to be carried out afresh on a new piece of tracing paper.

After drawing the design, and before you ink it in, it is always a good idea to take time to check through your work. And this can usefully include

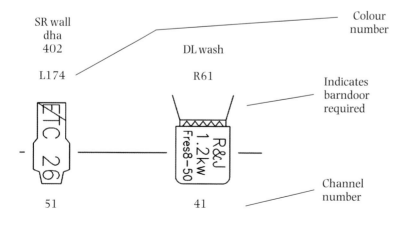

Lighting unit detail from a drawn design.

taking the drawing in to the venue (if you can), and making sure your visualization of the space has been correct, and that you have not put any equipment in the wrong place by making a basic mistake as to the dimensions or the relative position of things in the theatre.

The lighting designer will usually include a name plate labelling the plan by company, production director, designer and lighting designer, and the finish tracing is then taken to a printer for printing on to paper.

Computer-aided design (CAD)

Modern computer programs have been developed specifically with the drawing and listing of lighting designs in mind; they include AutoCad, Wysiwyg, Lightwrite and others. These programs provide clear and highly professional drawings and automatically generate much of the necessary paperwork – lantern and colour lists. In many cases these programs also have the added facility, variously successful, of allowing the lighting designer to 'see' what the lighting is going to look like! These 3D realizations are particularly useful for a number of things:

- Checking beam angles: checking to see if a unit will do what it is required to do – for example, is it big enough?
- Checking the distortion of the beam as it hits the playing area.
- Checking that the units, as placed in the venue, can light what is required of them – or, are they going to hit bits of set before they reach the areas they are aimed at?
- Showing the lighting designer the arrangement and movement of intelligent lighting cues (*see* pages 71–3)

What these programmes do not allow – so far – is a full colour realization of the lighting as imposed (for example) on a rehearsal. Whilst such computer graphics are no longer beyond the bounds of technical possibility, the cost in time and money to provide them remains prohibitive.

Summary

It should hopefully be obvious from this section that without the often seemingly tiresome need for bits of paper (or computer discs), the complex and detailed information that makes up a modern lighting design could easily become confused. And in an industry where time is money (and in which industry isn't this the case?), and where the lighting designer is always going to work best if they can be both calm and collected, good communication and its associated paperwork is vital.

And it is also very important that the lighting designer develops an organised, clear and efficient system overall in order to produce and work on a drawn lighting design. Just as good and clear note-taking is vital at various points of the process, so it is only by having a sensible working method that the lighting designer can maximize their time and get the most out of the various opportunities that will present themselves. Clarity of process, just like clarity of thought, allows the lighting designer the freedom to work effectively.

In order to achieve what the lighting plan illustrates, as should by now have become clear, the lighting designer needs a thorough understanding of the available equipment, either in the theatre or in the hire catalogue; this, then, is the next subject for our study.

9 THE EQUIPMENT

LIGHTING INSTRUMENTS

Choosing the right equipment to use is naturally part of every artist's work – the right brushes, the right sculpting knife, the right paint, the right marble... Whether we dignify the role of the theatrical lighting designer with the term 'artist' or not (a debate for another time, perhaps), the principle remains the same.

The main tools at the disposal of the lighting designer are the instruments that project the light on to the stage – properly called luminaires, but more often than not actually referred to as 'lanterns'. A stage luminaire or lantern is basically a light bulb in a box with a reflective mirrored surface and (often) an array of lenses used to project the light from the bulb out of one end of the box and towards the stage. Basic stage lanterns fall into four simple categories, and they were developed, and are therefore defined, by the kind of light they provide for the stage. They can thus be listed as follows:

- precision instruments
- soft lights
- wash lights
- punch lights

In each category a number of different variations exists, but basically we can add to this list a more precise name for each generic lantern type, thus:

- Precision instruments = profile spot lights
- soft/fill lights = fresnel spot lights or PC spot lights

OPPOSITE: A dramatic moment from Hiawatha. *Lighting by Neil Fraser.*

- wash lights = floodlights
- beam lights = par units

Note: Most lanterns using a lens system are referred to as spot lights.

In addition to this list there are also two other types of equipment: units that provide rather unusual light, often for a very specified need, usually termed 'special effects units'; and the very modern, so-called 'intelligent lights' or 'moving lights'. To both these categories we will return, but it is best to start with the four groups that still undertake all the real 'leg work' of any lighting design.

The Profile Spot

Of all spot lights, the profile spot (sometimes also referred to as an 'ellipsoidal profile') is the more accurate user of glass lenses and therefore provides the most accurate work. It is also usually the most efficient conveyor of light in terms of quantity. This is because not only do the lenses in a profile unit allow the light to be clearly 'focused', but the precision of the unit also allows more light to be projected further. The basic relationship between the main parts of a profile unit are as illustrated overleaf.

Note the following:

- The lens system allows the light to be precisely focused at a certain point – the focal point. Any object placed in the beam at the focal point will also be focused sharply in the beam, for example a gobo. And in this case the image is usually inverted in all planes – left to right, top to bottom.
- Moving the lens in relation to the light source shifts the focal point, and thus the focus can be adjusted, soft or sharp.

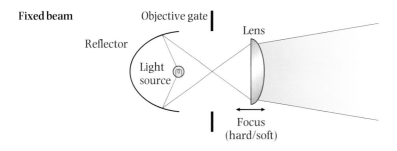

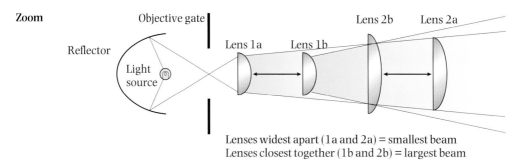

Lenses widest apart (1a and 2a) = smallest beam
Lenses closest together (1b and 2b) = largest beam

The profile spot.

The profile unit takes its name from its profile lens, and this in turn from the fact that it allows a beam of light to be focused, and thus an object placed in that beam to be clearly represented or 'profiled' in the beam of light. Because of its ability to focus upon an object clearly, the profile spot is the instrument that can also therefore precisely focus the light into a sharp circular (or ellipsoidal) pool, or be shaped by devices placed within the focal point.

The Zoom Profile
The illustration above shows how the movement of a single lens allows a beam of light to be focused soft or hard. It also shows that there is only one specific point where the focus is hard – it is only 'in focus' at a certain point of travel. In practice what this means is that the spotlight will only appear hard-edged at a certain size – the size dictated by the unit's focus, and the distance from the lantern to the stage. It is therefore known as a 'fixed beam

profile', and such fixed beam profiles are different-iated from each other by their beam angles – the angle of light that leaves the unit.

With a fixed beam unit, in order for a larger or smaller hard-edged beam of light to appear, the unit would have to be swapped for another instrument with a different focal length, or moved nearer or further from the stage. To alleviate this rather tedious problem, another lens can be added to our system, allowing the unit to then operate as a zoom profile – one where the focal point can be kept in place but the size of beam altered. The only drawback here is the fact that more lenses tend to mean more light loss, and less precision in the focusing.

Although the efficiency of profile spots has always relied on the light source used and the effectiveness of their lens systems, modern profile spots have become even more impressive with the use of axial bulb mountings and dichroic reflectors (*see* photographs opposite [top]).

*Modern profile spot
luminaries.*

The Fresnel Spot

These units have a lens designed to allow for optimum control over the *size* of the beam of light. In order to make a usable unit, as the diagram illustrates, the component parts of a much larger lens are packaged into a small and effective unit. In doing so, the ability of the curvature of the original lens to provide a range of very varying beam angles is cleverly preserved.

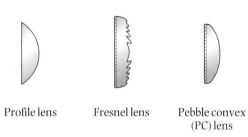

Profile lens   Fresnel lens   Pebble convex (PC) lens

Lens types

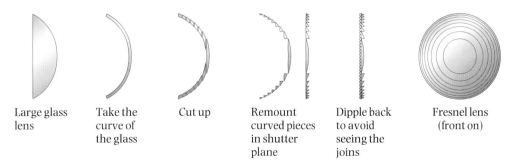

Large glass lens   Take the curve of the glass   Cut up   Remount curved pieces in shutter plane   Dipple back to avoid seeing the joins   Fresnel lens (front on)

Derivation of the fresnel lens.

However, this transformation is not without cost, because the fresnel lens no longer affords any precision in its focus, and its ability to 'profile' objects is so severely reduced that it is of no use whatsoever in this area. In fact the back of the lens is usually made with a dippled surface in order to further soften the beam, and to prevent any rings appearing in the light. Thus the fresnel becomes a unit specifically used to produce soft-edged beams of light with the ability to spot down very small, or to widen out to very large areas.

The PC Spot

A modern lantern developed to provide exactly the same effect as the older fresnel spot is the PC spot, which does involve a usually fairly hefty lens designed to provide a large range of beam angles – although with usually not as wide a range as the fresnel – but with a cleaner, more efficient light output.

'PC' stands for 'pebble convex', and this describes the lens shape and its dippled or pebbled rear surface, the latter designed to provide a fully softened beam of light.

The Flood

The flood unit derives from the earliest stage-lighting units and is therefore very simple. It consists of a bulb and reflector only, and it simply directs a fixed, unfocusable beam of light to the stage. The lack of lens means that the light output is not concentrated into a beam in any way, and thus the light leaving a flood does exactly what its name suggests and floods all over a very large area.

The rather uncontrollable nature of the output of a floodlight means it has rather limited use in a stage production – it has, of course, rather more use for sports events or other large outdoor activities, where large areas need lighting in a very basic, straightforward way. However, there is one particular area on stage where it can be useful, namely when large areas of light need to be provided for large stage cloths. A large cloth or area of stage flattage at the rear of a theatre, or even the back wall of the theatre itself, is referred to as a 'cyclorama', and thus specific floods have been developed to light this, called 'cyc' floods.

Cyc floods are made to produce light that will generally favour the vertical over the horizontal. They are made and are described in two ways, as symmetrical or asymmetrical. The latter provides a beam of light that is stronger to one end of its vertical range, thus allowing it to light a cloth efficiently whether placed at the bottom or top of it (*see* illustration opposite [top]).

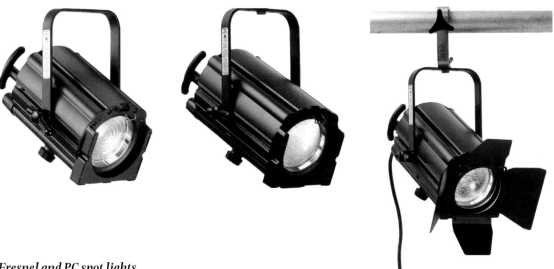

Fresnel and PC spot lights.

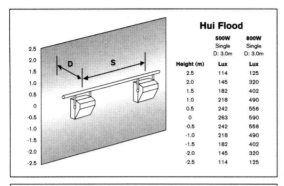

Hui Flood

Height (m)	500W Single D: 3.0m Lux	800W Single D: 3.0m Lux
2.5	114	125
2.0	145	320
1.5	182	402
1.0	218	490
0.5	242	556
0	263	590
-0.5	242	556
-1.0	218	490
-1.5	182	402
-2.0	145	320
-2.5	114	125

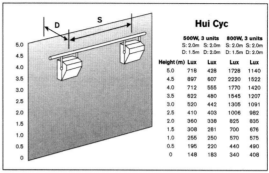

Hui Cyc

Height (m)	500W, 3 units S: 2.0m D: 1.5m Lux	500W, 3 units S: 2.0m D: 2.0m Lux	800W, 3 units S: 2.0m D: 1.5m Lux	800W, 3 units S: 2.0m D: 2.0m Lux
5.0	718	428	1728	1140
4.5	897	607	2220	1522
4.0	712	555	1770	1420
3.5	622	480	1545	1207
3.0	520	442	1305	1091
2.5	410	403	1006	982
2.0	360	338	825	835
1.5	308	281	700	676
1.0	255	250	570	575
0.5	195	220	440	490
0	148	183	340	408

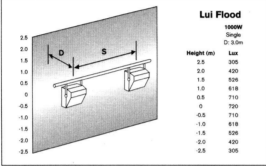

Lui Flood

Height (m)	1000W Single D: 3.0m Lux
2.5	305
2.0	420
1.5	526
1.0	618
0.5	710
0	720
-0.5	710
-1.0	618
-1.5	526
-2.0	420
-2.5	305

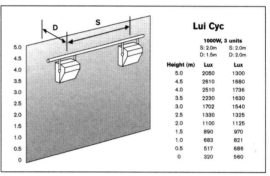

Lui Cyc

Height (m)	1000W, 3 units S: 2.0m D: 1.5m Lux	1000W, 3 units S: 2.0m D: 2.0m Lux
5.0	2050	1300
4.5	2610	1680
4.0	2510	1736
3.5	2230	1630
3.0	1702	1540
2.5	1330	1325
2.0	1100	1125
1.5	890	970
1.0	683	821
0.5	517	686
0	320	560

Technical specifications for symmetrical and asymmetrical flood units.

Single and batten flood light units.

Par 64 bulbs of varied beam angles.

The parcan.

The Beamlight and the Par

The beamlight is a unit designed to do what its name suggests: produce a narrow, powerful beam of light. The traditional unit is one that uses two reflectors, rather than lenses to fully concentrate the beam. Whilst this type of unit is still used on occasion, the more modern par unit has really overtaken it as the unit of choice for powerful, intense beams of light.

A par unit is based on the development of a fixed beam unit – a combination of lens, reflector and source – designed to provide the rock concert arena with an instrument capable of projecting a powerful beam of light, both intense white or highly coloured. Basically the par unit is a means to provide for a stage the intensity of an aircraft landing light, and the unit designed to hold the fixed beam unit is the parcan.

The par unit that a parcan holds is a par 64 (other size pars are used in many other contexts:

see below), and it comes in a variety of beam angles, from very narrow to wide. An unusual feature of the parcan beam is its oval shape, caused by the manner in which the internal light source is placed within the unit.

Other Par Lamps

The par 64 lamp is the theatre industry standard fixture, but it is itself merely one of a range of similar lighting units produced for many and varied uses outside the theatre industry. You may well have a par lamp in your house or garden. The chosen theatre unit is the par 64, so named after the diameter of its lens – at the imperial measure of 64 twelfths of an inch – thus the par 36 is proportionally smaller in diameter. Some of these units are used in theatre-type instruments – the par 36 is to be found in the bullet beam unit, and requires a transformer to connect it to the mains.

The Birdy

Another useful unit, and not unlike a par, is the birdy. This very small unit, with its 12-volt M16 'bulb', is commonly used on stage nowadays where space is tight because it produces a bright beam from a comparatively small unit. M16s come in a variety of beam angles and can be interchanged.

Discharge Units

At the other end of the scale from the humble birdy is a range of units that provide very powerful sources and are often rather large as a result. These units use as their light source the spark of light that is created as a powerful electrical current arcs across between two conductors. The first type of this unit was the carbon arc lantern, and it actually pre-dated the filament units that make up the rest of the range of theatre lighting equipment as described above; it also saw the demise of limelight as the brightest light source available in the theatre.

Discharge units are usually named after the combination of materials used within the 'bulb': CSI stands for 'compact source iodide', and HMI is 'hygerium metallic iodide'. These light sources turn up in a number of different units – or profiles – often those customized to operate as follow-spots, large floods and fresnels, and also in various of the intelligent light units available.

The distinct characteristics of discharge units, with their brilliant light output of an intense and pure quality, is the reason why they may be favoured for inclusion in a lighting design. As such they are often used in large theatres, for example as followspots in opera houses, where the distance from front-of-house to stage is quite considerable. Also in large theatres where a dramatic statement is required from a single or very few sources; again, this is also often characteristic of opera (*see* page 162).

Two particular features occur with these units, both due to the nature of the light source: first the arc units cannot be dimmed by conventional electronic means, and therefore either simply stay on, or are mechanically dimmed using internal or external shutters – sometimes with varying degrees of smoothness! The other feature of these units is

the colour of their light. It is not the same as that of the more conventional (often called 'generic') tungsten-filamented light source, usually being bluer in tone. Although this may be the reason for the choice of unit, there also exists a range of gels available to correct the colour to match that of tungsten, and these clearly indicate the shift in colour that the light from these units creates (*see* illustration overleaf).

EQUIPMENT USAGE

The description of the main lighting instruments should give the reader some idea as to their various merits, and therefore how much they are likely to be used. The profile is used for distance and accuracy, the fresnel and PC for adding washes and cover, the flood for cyc work, and the par for its power and attack (*see* the examples on pages 97, 164 and 171).

However, it must never be forgotten that all these lanterns are actually just fairly basic

The birdy and birdy lamp.

instruments for pushing light in a specific direction, and that many of them can be used to supplement or substitute for the other. For example, a tightly focused fresnel can do just as good a job as a soft-focused profile; or a widely focused fresnel could also make quite a good job of covering a cyclorama with colour. What is important is that the lighting designer gets plenty of experience in the using of equipment, so they can make their own decisions about what type of lantern they like for what job. Certainly strict adherence to some sort of prescribed usage does not suggest much flexibility or imagination.

Peripheral Lantern Equipment

This section concerns what peripheral lantern equipment does, and how it works.

Gobo

Simple or detailed metal or glass shapes that are manufactured to interface with the beam of light from a unit (usually a profile spot) in order to project an image on to stage.

Iris

A device that allows the beam of light to be reduced in size but preserves its circular shape. The iris does this by simply blocking the light within the unit.

Doughnut/donut

A device fitted to the front of a unit (usually a profile spot) to reduce the number of images being produced from the unit in order to clean up the image – therefore used in particular in combination with gobos.

Barndoor

A shutter device that fixes to the front of a unit (usually a fresnel, PC, parcan or flood, all basic units except the profile spot, which uses internal shutter sets) to provide a mechanical means to control the spill and shape of the beam of light.

Tophat

A cylindrical device that fixes to the front of a unit (usually to restrict spill and size of the beam – and in the case of the parcan also to change its typically oval beam into a more circular one.

Gel

The name for the basic colour medium used in stage units; it functions as follows: 'white light' passes through a colour medium (gel or filter) to

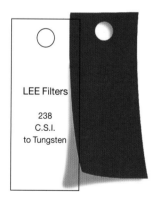  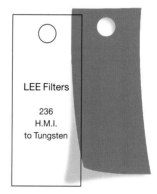

Colour correction filters. Note: Remember that these gels show the correction required for the discharge units to be adjusted to resemble a tungsten light source – the amount of pink indicates how much bluer the discharge unit is and therefore how much pink has to be added to its beam just so it looks like conventional tungsten light beam. Tungsten light itself is much warmer – more orange in appearance – than daylight, as the colour correction to convert it to daylight clearly shows.

become coloured; as part of this process, some light output is lost.

Note 1. Manufacturers' swatch books often contain information about the loss of intensity/ light transmission, and the mixture of colours that have gone to make up the colour in question.

Note 2. Dark colours significantly reduce the light intensity from the lighting instrument.

Dichroic colour production differs from conventional gel in that colour is manufactured within the instrument (usually an 'intelligent light') by defraction. The different wave-lengths of colour are split up via prisms, and only part is allowed through into the beam (*see also* the colour section on page 29).

Scroller
This is the most common add-on unit to provide colour changing for a basic 'generic' (non-intelligent) unit. A scroller fits on the front of a unit (typically a parcan or fresnel), and contains a scroll of colours that can unwind to a prescribed position in front of the light beam and are stored on either side of the unit as a roll.

Other Equipment: Special Effects Units
A number of lighting devices have been specially developed over the years to provide very particular types of light. These units have their very own, specific jobs to do, and whilst, like all lighting sources, new and innovative uses can be found for them, they are on the whole less flexible and thus less used than the basic lighting equipment previously discussed. The most common units are as follows:

Animation wheels
These provide a flickering in the light source of varying degrees; often combined with gobos and colour, they mimic the rippling of water or flame.

Gobo rotators/yo-yos
These allow the fixed image of a gobo to be rotated or moved backwards and forwards within the beam of light; they are particularly effective in combination with animation wheels.

Projected wheel effects
Black and white or coloured glass wheels that depict specific things and move in front of the light source. Lenses allow for degrees of sharpness (focusing) and size. Typical examples are clouds, water effects, rain, snow and suchlike.

Strobe
A flashing source of light with a clear and distinct on/off action, with no fade up or down times. Used famously to cheat the look of slow motion on stage, or other various harsh attacking effects, for example lightning, warfare.

Mirror balls
Usually rotating multi-reflectors of light – the old ballroom favourite.

Scanners
Disco effect, bright lights in motion.

UV: Ultra violet light, or 'black light'
Provided by a UV strip or floodlight, and allowing certain substances to reflect the UV colour. These units can play a major part in transformation scenes, as they can instantly reveal 'hidden' aspects of a setting, costume or make-up.

Intelligent Lights
So-called intelligent units – or 'moving lights' as they are perhaps more accurately called – come in many varieties, although generally speaking there are two main types: those where the entire lighting unit moves on various motored yokes to point in whatever direction is required; and those that stay static and rely on redirecting the beam of light by the use of a mirror on gimbles. Motorized yokes are also available that allow 'generic' units to be motor-driven.

Generally speaking, intelligent units, whilst very versatile in their ability to be refocused and re-pointed at the touch of a button, do not actually add anything to the lighting arena – they simply replace the more conventional equipment. That is to say, they can be hard- or soft-focused, large or small, shuttered or goboed, and change colour just like the equipment we have already discussed. This is, of course, not to underplay their increasing use as an effective solution to stage-lighting problems.

Intelligent lights are, by their very nature, quite complex beasts, and one of the great myths that came with their inception was the idea that they would make life easier and save time. Along with that other great myth of technological advance, that a computerized world would produce a paper-free office, this has not proved the case. These units need proper preparation, and they take time to plot and use. Once incorporated within a design, however, they can more than prove their worth. Along with the units themselves has evolved a plethora of control systems dedicated to making their use as effective as possible, and the creation of complex CAD systems to help plot their use and exploit their enormous potential for moving as part of a continuous dancing architectural accompaniment to such events as, for example, rock concerts.

In theatrical use, intelligent lights, even when the actual movement of the light is unseen, with their ability to refocus, recolour, reshape, or replace a light on a stage, make for almost limitless possibilities. And herein lies a problem, because it becomes only too easy to overuse these units once they are installed, and thereby lose sight of

any purity within a design. Care must be taken at all times to make sure the dramatic action of a piece drives the lighting, and *not the other way round*.

LIGHTING CONTROLS

The other main piece of equipment essential to the work of the lighting designer is that used to control lighting units. Lighting controls are one of the main instruments in modern times to benefit from the development of computer technology, and as such have become highly refined and sophisticated. However, this is not to say that they are overly complex to use or understand – after all, they were conceived on the notion of making the lighting designer's life easier.

Controls come in many variations, the main ones being concerned with the following:

* The type of performance, whether stage show, rock concert, fixed exhibition or conference, and therefore...
* ...whether human interface or fully automated operation is necessary, which would dictate the permanence of the installation – a few weeks, months or years. And also therefore...
* ...the complexity required – whether a few cues

Non-Theatrical Light Sources

Although the equipment described in this chapter represents the mainstay of most theatre lighting, there is no real reason why any source cannot be used, and indeed some lighting designers have built their reputations on the use of alternative light sources. Examples include fluorescent light, industrial arc lights, ultra violet light, and so on; in the right setting nothing is more effective than real candlelight.

Whilst there are health and safety issues with some natural light sources – fire, for example! – there are also technical issues with some of

them, the lack of dimming ability being an obvious example. Nevertheless, experimentation with alternative sources can be very rewarding – although it must also be remembered that the use of gel and special effects with conventional units is specifically designed to provide the lighting designer with the means to reproduce just these effects!

Some units have become so popularly used that they have been adopted as part of the conventional kit, and indeed the parcan is probably the best example of this, and the birdy another.

ABOVE: A motorized wash light – the VL5 by VariLight.

ABOVE RIGHT AND BELOW: The spectacular effect of a large moving light rig and stage mist.

or hundreds, simple cross-fades or complex special effects.

- The extent of immediate hands-on individual control required for each power output, potentially to each unit.
- The type of units being controlled, whether generic units or intelligent lights.

In practice, most control units are now computer-based machines, the working of which varies depending on the software in use or installed. As such, even the most basic control units can be utilized to control sophisticated systems if necessary, the limitation here being based on available memory and ease of use.

Controls can also be divided into the following basic types:

- **Manual**: Where each output has its own individual fader, and faders can be grouped into presets, and therefore scenes. The operator works from listed cues, showing what faders (or channels) are required for each scene, and at what output level, and how to get from scene to scene, this latter being either to work in a 'live' preset or 'cross fade' from preset to preset. It is usual for a manual board to have two or three presets.

- **Memory**: Whereby lighting states can be recorded and played back at the press of a button from a computer memory. Such machines typically allow the operator to record timings, run individual cues or sequences, run special effects, and so on. Such controls usually still require an operator to trigger a cue or sequence of cues, but the change between lighting states (the cross-fade) or a sequence of cross-fades is then controlled by the machine itself. This allows for split timings, delayed operation of part of a cue, automatic follow-on cues, the reshaping of dimmer profiles, intelligent light resetting, and many other useful complexities (*see* pages 81 and 82).

- **Intelligent**: Memory lighting desks devoted to the operation of units with multi-functions (called attributes) – these dedicated controls allow for easier hands-on presetting and control of the sophisticated intelligent units. For example, allocating preset patterns to the movement, and visualizing the position of the units on the board mimic, and allowing for touch control of units from this mimic. In all, this machine will allow faster manipulation of these specific types of units.

Summary

The description of the equipment in this chapter is intended to illustrate just how simple these devices are – the light-producing units themselves are fairly straightforward, and even the more sophisticated control systems are easy to understand. The relative simplicity of this equipment – the lighting designer's basic toolkit – helps to make the process of using it likewise clear and straightforward.

More information directly linked to the use of this equipment can be found in the next chapter, as it deals with rigging, focusing and plotting (pages 75 and 78).

With our knowledge of the equipment we are to use, and with our drawn lighting design from Chapter 8, we are now ready to move from theory to practice, and from page to stage.

10 THE TASK IN PRACTICE

THE RIG

Once a lighting designer has committed their work to paper, the job of organizing and achieving the physical reality of this paperwork devolves to the technical team, and in particular the lighting department. This department on any production is usually under the control of a chief or production electrician (more often now called the head of lighting, or the lighting director, or something similar). Whilst keeping in touch with the lighting designer, it is the job of this team to take the relevant information and get the lighting rig to a point where the lighting designer can begin to achieve their vision in the focusing session. The role of the assistant lighting designer, who may well come into play here, is discussed on page 11.

This team takes the drawn lighting design from the lighting designer, and translates it onto stage. Equipment is prepared and corralled, colour cut and framed, gobos ordered and put in holders, and then all is brought together in the 'rigging session', at the end of which all equipment has been put in place, plugged up, tested and is ready to focus.

It is not really necessary or usual for the lighting designer to be at the rigging session – their art comes into play from the focus session onwards. However, if you can be in attendance, this might be helpful so you can offer advice; and even if you do not stay for the whole session, it is a good idea to be available, even by telephone. The team is always working against a finite time to get the rig done, and any problems that the lighting designer can answer immediately may help save time later – and unforeseen things can always happen.

Towards the end of the session it is also a good idea for the lighting designer to look over the rig to see what problems they can foresee, some of which may be correctable there and then; and also to remind themselves of what the rigged equipment is there to do. In the time between drawing and rigging, the lighting designer may have begun to forget some of the nuances of the intended design, and viewing the physical rig in place is as good a place as any to start recalling them.

THE FOCUS

As the lighting designer arrives at the focusing session they have to be ready to take control of the team. Focusing consists of directing the lighting team who, under instruction, will go from unit to unit and point each one where you want it, and in the manner you want it. The lighting designer will usually work from the plan or their separate notes. Obviously it is vital that the lighting designer knows exactly what they are doing – time is precious in these sessions – and this only comes about from good and thorough preparation, which in turn should have resulted in clear and thorough notes (whether in the head or on paper). The following points are also important to bear in mind:

Focus Tips
- Make a considered decision as to where to start in the rig: *easiest place first* will get a good momentum going, but *hardest place first* will get rid of the worst things while you and the team are still fresh. It is your call.
- Keep your team busy and thus the pace going; try and make sure they are always ready when you are, and keep them informed about where you want to work next.
- Keep your directions to the team simple and direct: 'Move it to your right – put it here

Work alongside your team and keep your directions clear.

[indicating with your hand or foot] – bigger – smaller – softer – harder', and so on.

- Once under way, credit the team with enough intelligence to be able to achieve a lot of the elements of the focusing for you – so tell them what you are trying to achieve with any lantern, and allow them to match other pre-focused units.
- Make sure you give the team breaks – they will work better for it – but do not let these become too prolonged. It is all about pace.
- Even if things are not going to plan, and you are worrying about where you have placed certain units, keep the mood light: your team will work better for you if they do not become stressed or worried by your fears.
- On the other hand, along with keeping up the pace, also keep the mood business-like and organized.
- Do, however, take time, when necessary, to think through what you are doing – do not rush things. There is little worse in this session than having to go back to a unit because you have forgotten something relevant. But if this has to be done, do not shy away from doing it, either.

- Do not leave a hundred and one things to repair later, because 'later' may not happen!
- Remember the problems of the focuser; for example, only have the unit turned on at the last moment so that it does not get too hot too soon. Give them time to do their job – but also expect well paced work.

As you can see, a lot of these notes concern themselves with *clarity of intent*, combined with keeping up a *good pace*. There are also specific focusing rules that can be applied to the actual action itself.

How to Focus a Lantern

- Before starting, be clear in your mind as to what you want the unit to achieve, and how it fits into the whole pattern of the design.
- It is usual to start with the unit spotted down – as small as possible – in order to see clearly where the light is and where it is centred. However, do not feel bound to do this on every occasion, because if its place is clear to you, it will only waste time to make it small, only to make it big again. Also, if it is only another unit in a group that you have already focused, you should know what size it needs to be – so go straight to it.
- It is usual to focus each unit on its own, with only that one illuminated. This allows you to see clearly what it is doing. However, once again you will not want to follow this rule always, as comparing units and adding to washes and the like, can be just as easily achieved by using the units you have already focused as guides.
- However, having focused elements of the rig, resist the temptation to begin putting together lighting states, as this will only hold you up and waste time.
- It is very important to remember when focusing to allow for the height of the actor or set – do not focus to the floor.
- It is usual to show the focuser where you want the light by standing on stage and saying 'on me here'. However, having done this, move away, and try not to focus the unit by being in the light, as this can lead to two things: blinding yourself,

and not really being able to see what the light is actually doing.
- You can use a member of the crew to 'stand' for you, in place of the actor – but in actual fact you should not need this, and once again it is likely to make the process take longer. Naturally when you have been doing this job for a while, habits will form – so make sure they are good ones!
- Having placed the unit, the order of events usually follows this pattern: size, focus (soft or hard), and then shape (with shutters or barndoors).
- Check all aspects of the unit – not just the light being where you want it to be – check for spill, and other unforeseeable things. To do this, stand back from the unit and look at all its edges.
- When you have finished with the unit, make sure it is 'locked off', so that it will not move if slightly jolted later. This is especially important on a flown or suspended bar.
- With each unit you focus you will learn more about how the overall operation is working, and this should allow you to speed up, to keep an eye on the 'big picture'.
- It is usual to focus with the colour in place, but if a particularly dark colour is being used it can be difficult to see its extremes, so ask for it to be removed whilst you are focusing, and replaced when you are finished.
- When focusing paired units, if possible, ask for the other unit to be unplugged or pointed away while you focus – make your life as easy as you can.

The act of focusing can make or break a good lighting design, and it is well named as the lighting designer needs to be clearly 'focused' on the job to make sure it is done well and efficiently.

It is also important to make sure that unexpected 'bonuses' or 'gifts' of lighting are not missed or left unexploited. Unforeseen things often happen that even the best prepared and planned lighting design cannot account for. It is, after all, extremely difficult, even for the most seasoned practitioner, to fully realize in the mind how the two-dimensional world of the lighting plan, or even the three-dimiensional world of their imagination, is actually going to work in real life. So when units are lit that are pointing randomly (as left by the rigging team) and yet produce lighting that amazes, then these things must be noted and thought through. Thus, if the effect they are creating is going to enhance the overall lighting of the production, and if placing the unit (or new units) to utilize this unexpected bonus does not undermine the work that also has to be done and has been planned for, then use them. In addition, even whilst focusing, the mind, intent on the job in hand, can also afford to be exploring and testing what is being created in order that any extras can be included that may also enhance the lighting.

Problem Solving during Focusing

Problems will always occur when focusing, as the operation of lighting any show of size is both complex and unpredictable. The main enemy here is time, so the decision either to solve the problem there and then, or later, is often dependent on what will be the quickest solution. Taking time to think things through is a luxury that one cannot always afford. Of course the problems can be myriad, and the ability to think fast on one's feet cannot be underestimated.

As a general rule it is important to keep going – pace, again – so use your team well. There should be someone available to sort out problems while you continue to focus. In an ideal world you should have more than one person focusing for you, in order that they can take it in turns and be getting the next unit ready or into place as you do the one before. Nevertheless, it may be necessary to sacrifice this luxury in order that one of them troubleshoots the rig. Hopefully your head of team will also not have put themselves into a position whereby they are too busy, and so they, too, should be available to help and advise.

PLOTTING AND CUES

Like charting a great voyage across the oceans or skies of the world, the act of creating the lighting for every part of a production is called 'plotting'.

Thus it is necessary to plot one's course through a performance from one lighting cue to the next (the same will, of course, be true of all other technical aspects of the production) and, in doing so, record this journey so that it can be repeated over and over again.

Plotting usually occurs just before the technical rehearsal. The 'tech' is when all aspects of the production are put together and rehearsed, with the action. During the plotting, for every different moment of lighting within the piece, levels are set, timings given, and the overall moods delicately constructed.

Plotting is an act of creativity, and the crucial moment when the ideas of the lighting designer are finally fully revealed and put forward for consideration. It can thus be a potentially very stressful and fraught occasion. Because of this, once again, all the preparation beforehand must go towards alleviating this potential tension. In this case this includes having discussed in detail with the director what is required, and having produced it in the focusing. Alongside having good notes and a clear plan to work from, the lighting designer must also be perfectly lucid during this session in two ways: firstly, to the control operator(s), so that the lighting can be plotted quickly and recorded efficiently; and secondly, to the director, so that they understand what they are being asked to look at.

A certain amount of bravura and bluff is often needed in these sessions, because unless the lighting designer has been able to pre-plot, this is often also the first time they have really been able to assemble the lighting themselves, and therefore they are also having to decide whether certain combinations are working or not. Naturally displaying any doubt in this matter does not necessarily help the director decide. What this comes down to is the need to lead the director to a positive conclusion, even when you yourself have doubts. Remember, you are the expert in this field, and this can often mean that you are also a better judge of the visual than the director – they can too often be 'bogged down' in the text. So keep positive, and work out your own issues whilst beaming positive rays of approval to the director! On the other hand, a certain level of frankness will be necessary when things are patently not being effective. Finding the right balance here can be every bit as tricky as calling the lighting levels and plotting the cues themselves.

Before starting the plot it is a good idea for the lighting designer to 'flash through' the rig (looking at every unit) before the director arrives to remind them of everything it contains – it is surprisingly easy to forget things under the pressure of a formal plotting session.

Remember also that neither the director nor anyone else necessarily expects you to be able to go straight to the finished plot for each cue – degrees of discussion and experimentation are allowed. In fact often the director will be much happier if this is the case, as it will allow them to be part of the process more fully. However, directors can also expect seemingly ridiculous things at this session – often it is as if the lighting control has a button for every possibility: buttons marked 'creepier', 'weirder', or even 'unforeseen request'!

Obviously in such cases you have to make the best of what you are being asked for – or,

after having listened thoroughly, explain that as this was something you had not talked about previously, it will take some time to think out and include in the rig. In other words, give yourself time by promising to look into it. It is important here not to promise too much – as time will, by necessity, not allow for too many major changes – and although it goes against the grain, you are allowed to say things such as 'No, that won't be possible', or even 'I don't think that's a good idea – let's not do that.' At all events, be positive and be clear.

When unexpected things do require solutions, it is surprising how taking a little time away from the pressures of the plotting makes finding them so much easier. Although it is good to think on one's feet, it is also difficult to keep a good overview in such a pressured session. Indeed 'flashing through' the rig even in mid-plot (perhaps during a break) can reveal surprising things to the lighting designer that in the heat of the moment they have forgotten – for instance, the unit that was meant as a special for Act 1 but wasn't needed, can easily

Lighting designer at the production desk.

supply that unforeseen special that was asked for in Act 5.

There are various ways to start a plotting session, and, along with the lighting designer, the director themselves may have a preference. Here are the major variations:

- 'Flash through' the rig for the director, explaining how all the units will be used, and how they fit into what has been discussed.
- In the same way, show the director prepared groups of units – front light, back light, colour washes, gobo effects, and so on.
- Simply start with the first lighting cue – usually the pre-set – and move on through the play cue by cue.
- Start with the most important lighting cue, and having defined this, move on to others – thus not necessarily plotting cues in the order in which they will appear.

It may be the case that the formal plotting session, as it appears on the production schedule, is not actually used with the intention of creating the final lighting plot. After all, it is very common to make many changes during the technical rehearsals, and therefore quite often only a 'rough sketch' of the lighting states is made in the plot.

It is useful, however, to have the actual number of cues, their place in the play, and a rough timing for each, established at this point. In the plotting session the cue points are put into 'the book' – the master copy of the script – by the deputy stage manager (DSM). It is from 'the book' that the dsm will cue all aspects of the production.

Rules for Plotting

Pre-Plot
- Arrange a pre-plotting session (i.e. without the director) whenever possible – but do not become too attached to anything you create in the pre-plot, as the director will naturally want their say. Better to use this time not to create final states, but to...

- Use pre-plotting time to 'learn' your rig – to find out what it can do.
- Pre-plot useful groups of units to save time – for example colour washes, covers etc. Remember to make these groups as useful as possible by balancing the units within them – do not necessarily just use everything in a group at the same level.
- Do not adhere too rigidly to these groups.

The Plot
- Always be clear in what you are trying to achieve.
- Remember you are part of a team, and do not be afraid to ask for creative and technical assistance or opinions if you need them.
- Explain (persuasively) and clearly what you are doing or aiming at as you plot: do not expect those around you to be mind-readers.
- Use levels that allow for adjustment.
- If a thing does not work, move on (but remember what you have left unused or have discarded).
- *Keep good notes.*
- Remain flexible and open to new ideas...
- But also take time to explain yours.
- Explore *all* the possibilities of your rig.
- Set rough timings; they can usually be refined later.
- Make the timings fit the action or mood; the fastest cue will not be abrupt if it fits the action. Likewise a cue a second late can be a disaster!
- As a general rule, fast timings are dramatic, slow ones subtle.
- However, all cues only work in the right dramatic context.
- Make sure the operators are plotting your lighting properly, and *get it saved and backed up*. And make sure that any written notes (for example, cue sheets) are likewise copied, with one set always on hand.
- Remember the lighting *always* looks better in the full action of the play, and everything can always be changed later! So...
- *Keep calm*: the rule here is, there will always be time to panic later!

The DSM at the prompt desk, cueing from 'the book'.

Building Cues

As indicated above, when building cues it is a good idea to start with levels that allow for upward adjustment. But most importantly, and in addition to this, it is also a good idea to start with the core of the intended cue – the thing that is most important about it. In many cases this will be the key light, around which the rest of the cue should be dressed.

In a 'general cover' (*see* page 53) it may well be the backlight that should be your starting point. But wherever you do start, do not make the mistake of thinking that the light that will be illuminating the actor's face is the most important in this. Naturally it is often of vital importance – we do need to see the actors – but if this book has taught us nothing else, it is that this light source is rarely the brightest or the most vital for our lighting.

Plotting Techniques

The more sophisticated that lighting becomes, the more we need to use the equipment at our disposal to its fullest extent. Below are a few such sophisticated elements:

Split timings

Cues cross-fade one to another over time, but often times can be overlapped by using different up and down times. This can vastly improve the look and effectiveness of a cross-fade. The uptime of a cue dictates the speed of units entering or increasing in value from one cue to the next, the downtime those units decreasing in value or leaving the cue entirely.

A faster uptime often creates a smoother cross-fade. However, a faster downtime can create a useful dip in order to punctuate the action. It all depends on what you want.

Fade types

There are other types of cue than the cross-fade, for example the **move-fade**. This allows for cues to be operated one upon another independently, and is specifically used when cues need to run concurrently. As lighting designer you merely have to ask if the control can do what you want it to – although a good knowledge of what is possible is always a good thing.

Pre-heats

Units that come up late in a cue can be pre-heated in the previous cue at an unseen level. Similarly, units that fade out too fast can be post-heated in the next cue. Thus a cue can be smoother, with units appearing 'in sync' with each other and the cue appearing slower without actually having to change the timing.

Unseen cues

A play may have any number of 'unseen' cues, used to subtly change the mood, or accommodate changes on stage. Therefore do not always feel that a cue must be updated – if a cue has worked well for the scene already, simply add the new adjustment as a new cue. This works especially when the new cue is simply to place light where it is now needed, and not to make a dramatic point. Remember this only works if the cues remain unseen by the audience. All seen cues must be logical and have dramatic motivation, otherwise they will simply make no sense.

Developing and Refining Cues

The Technical Rehearsal

After the plotting session the production usually moves into the technical rehearsal. In this session all the elements of the play are put together, as each section or cue sequence is run with the full company on stage. These sections start and stop in order to iron out any problems until, when they run perfectly, the 'tech' can move on to the next sequence.

This session is then usually followed by a number of full dress rehearsals of the play. Again, everything is run through on stage, but this time without stopping (hopefully!).

During the 'tech' it is important that the lighting designer utilizes every moment to refine and perfect the cues and cue sequences. As always, this involves the taking of good notes, but also the ability to make changes quickly 'on the hoof'. The number of changes is different on each occasion, and partly depends on how rough a plot has previously occurred. Changes can be minor or major – for example, adding a second to a timing, 10 per cent to a unit level, or completely re-plotting a cue, adding or subtracting cues, and so on. A good working relationship with the deputy stage manager – the person charged with calling all the cues – is, of course, essential in this.

The action during a 'tech' can be stopped by any number of problems, and the lighting designer is one of the team allowed to bring things to a halt. However, if every little thing is allowed to bring things shuddering to a standstill, then it is probable that the 'tech' will overrun. Thus it is good to develop the ability to work quickly whilst the action is running, only stopping when absolutely necessary, and modern lighting boards in particular allow for this.

Dress Rehearsals

It is usual to have a number of dress rehearsals (two or three is typical), with notes coming from each session that allow us to further refine the work. The notes from director, designer and ourselves are worked on between each dress rehearsal, with the idea that the final 'dress' will be the finished product – though naturally on very busy productions this is not always the case, and first nights can be fraught. Special care therefore must be taken in the final session not to make any foolish mistakes that will only be revealed on the first night.

All through this process the taking of good notes is vital, and in order to allow the lighting designer to keep their eye on the action before them, and therefore off their notepads, it is useful to develop a shorthand – though in doing so make sure the notes remain legible. Make sure that you are well positioned to take notes, with a light and a plan beside you, and anything else you may need. It is not unusual to have a remote monitor showing you the cues being executed, and a headset so you can hear them being called by the deputy stage manager – and to communicate with if really necessary. Number each note, and draw a line under each one to separate it from the next.

Here are some examples of shorthand:

Q5 c14 10↑ which means, in cue 5 raise channel 14 by 10%

_____

Q12 = 10s↑7↓ which means, in cue 12 make the timing up in 10 seconds, down in 7 seconds.

_____

C6 → which means, move channel 6 to the right.

Summary

After the dress rehearsals comes the big night – the opening of the show – and it is vitally important for our sanity that the last thing we do is enjoy the end result of our work. And then feel free to leave it behind (having learned new lessons as required from the experience), and move on to new and exciting challenges.

In the next section of this book the reader has the chance to stand beside the lighting designers as they undertake their work, each practical example or case study showing the methods and concepts that have been described in this book in use in the real world.

Case Studies: Lighting Design in Action

Understanding the concepts and processes of stage lighting is one thing: actually using them is quite another! The case studies that follow are about the process of design: the how, the why, the when, and the where of lighting design, and about how these design decisions are made. The pieces have been chosen to illustrate and expand on points already made in this book, and as such some are analysed in more detail than others. But all are concerned with the actual lighting – the ideas, the equipment, the creative challenge.

And so there is by necessity a shift of tone at this point in this book, and it is something that needs acknowledging so that it does not surprise and confuse the reader. It is because the rest of this book takes you into the mind of the lighting designer – indeed, the first of the case studies in this book takes a very personal look at the entire process of lighting design, from the first phone call to the first night – and because all of the case studies that follow are *real*: the events described actually took place, the people involved did their creative and technical best, and the productions were presented to an eager audience, with lighting making its usual important (vital) contribution.

In describing the process of lighting design it is important to stress that there are no universal solutions to problems. Hence the many different techniques that lighting designers use to achieve the same result – namely, to get the show lit. And often, as we shall see, when touring a show, the differing lighting positions can alter how the end result is achieved, as washes and angles change drastically – by circumstance rather than by design.

The lighting designer makes a series of choices on technical grounds in order eventually to please their designer's eye in the service of the production. It is these decisions that these case studies will examine, and in so doing discover along the way why any lamp, position or colour is chosen.

It is also true that on occasion in the theatre a lighting designer can find that all of their hard-wrought plans are not quite delivering, or indeed seem to be 'failing' in the eyes of the director. Even the best laid plans can go awry, and it is certainly always important for the lighting designer to be open to the way light actually works in the theatre – as opposed to how they thought it would work on paper!

To fully illustrate such events, anecdote will also have a role in these case studies; for example, to recall one lighting session for a new Glen Tetley dance piece for the Royal Ballet with **John B. Read** lighting: on stage was a backcloth, painted on which was a detailed and much appliquéd, vaguely turbulent sky. Due to the texture on the cloth, John began the session with various specials from the lighting bridge, and 'glanced' the light across the cloth from the wings, allowing for subtle changes and moods throughout the piece. When he returned the next day, after sleeping on what was not sitting quite right, he reverted to simply lighting the dancers and ignored the backdrop, letting it sit there while he pulled the mood and changes about on the stage space instead. His ability to see through what was there in front of him to the reality of what was really needed – in this case, nothing – is what puts John B. Read at the forefront of his profession.

So throughout these case studies we shall find the very simple question 'Just what do you actually hope to achieve with this lamp?' coming back to haunt us time and again.

Hindsight is, of course, always 20/20, and after having lit a production, you will necessarily reflect, and often realize that something could have been done differently or looked better. This, however, is more the reserve of personal reflection; certainly do not tell the chief on opening night that half the lamps were not needed! Every artist needs to know at what point they can say 'It is done', or 'Enough is enough', and move on to the next task.

Note: Throughout the following text, gel colours are noted by number and sometimes description. However, a full list of Rosco, Lee and GAM colours can be found at: lee.co.uk, gamcolor.com and rosco.com.

Setting up the tent in the Oxford Stage Company revival of The Contractor *by David Storey.*

11 LIGHTING FOR DRAMA

SCENES FROM AN EXECUTION BY HOWARD BARKER FOR DUNDEE REPERTORY THEATRE

THE INITIAL OFFER

People often ask, 'So how did you get that job?' And the answer, more often than not, is 'I got a phone call ...' Sometimes you know why, and sometimes not – and other times you know you'll never get a call again! On this occasion it was after the opening night of another project, and a message left from Dominic Hill, director of the Dundee Repertory Theatre Company: could I call him.

There are many reasons why lighting designers, and the whole gamut of other gifted technical personnel, work behind the scenes. It may be because they feel they are just not cut out for expressing themselves in front of more than three or four people at a time; and those who are probably want to be an actor anyway. So this kind of message pushes all the correct emotional buttons: you are flattered, you get worried about what to say, you choose the moment to call back very carefully. But call back you do, and soon. The conversation went along the lines of:

Hello, I really liked your work on...I was wondering if you'd be interested in lighting *Scenes from an Execution*...Howard Barker...Not often done...important revival, especially out of town...Almeida did it last, Glenda Jackson won an award...The theatre is to be converted from proscenium/thrust to an in-the-round space, and

OPPOSITE: **Scenes from an Execution.** *Lighting by Simon Bennison.*

I see the action as a series of painted scenes. I want the lighting to play a very important role in the piece...Would you be interested...Good, the dates are...Do you think you're available?

At this point we all eventually learn to say, 'I would love to, but I'm not quite sure what I'm doing during that week. If I can check my diary, I'll get back to you in the next couple of days...' And once the phone is down you are then free to do a small dance, punch the air, and utter a restrained, 'Yessss' – and then check nervously if the phone was really down when you made all those noises. When you discover it was, you reach for the diary, and then do it all again, when you discover that you are free.

The point here is that nerves, even at this early stage, are normal, but so is – and should be – the adrenalin rush of being wanted, and getting the opportunity to ply your trade, and hopefully do a very good job into the bargain. So also is the need to react positively to the phone call – but give yourself time to reflect as to whether you really want the job. After all, the timing may be less than perfect, the money rather indifferent, and so on; furthermore, stretching yourself too far – taking on too much – helps no one.

THE FIRST THEATRE VISIT

Speaking from Surrey, at one point in the conversation, the question was asked, 'So how exactly do I get to Dundee?' To which the reply was, 'It's fine, there is a direct flight from London

City Airport.' With this reply you know transport will be fine, and arrange the first theatre visit. The director also promises to send a script, which someone duly does on his behalf.

And so the twin propellers of the plane bank around the River Tay and touch down in Dundee, I jump into a taxi, and am eventually dropped off in Tay Square.

The Dundee Repertory Theatre is a fine theatre, the design its own but drawn heavily from sources such as the National Theatre's 'Olivier' and the Chichester Festival Theatre. It is a temple to breeze block, but somehow there is a calm to Dundee, and the building occupies its own space well: a feast of raw materials, with everything a producing theatre needs all on site.

Swiftly introduced to all, a meeting is soon in progress with the designer and director. At this juncture there is an interesting arrangement of politics and gamesmanship about to begin, which goes something like this: we are both there because of the director. The director wants us both there, but the designer has a closer relationship with the director by virtue of time. The designer knows he has to befriend the lighting designer because his set relies on him, but the director is not too fussed about all of that because he knows that it does not matter about the chair going here or the drape going there, because the lighting is going to make the piece work anyway, especially when in-the-round.

So we meet and chat, and offer up opinions – but points of view not too strong or committed – and you walk off with a bunch of notes and drawings, knowing that it all has a good chance of changing. During this visit – the first look inside the theatre – the opportunity to study the volume and architecture of the stage space can be much more important.

READING THE PLAY AND STARTING DESIGN

Whilst studying in America under Jennifer Tipton (Professor of Lighting Design at Yale University), each week we were given a play to read, and then had to talk about it during the following Monday lighting seminar. The class was huge, and contained not only lighting students but designers, dramaturgs, directors, costume designers, and so on, and it was these people who were often the ones to speak during the seminar, leaving the thoughtful would-be lighting designers with their thoughts, nodding and absorbing.

The colour G842 in use during the show.

Generally everyone agreed with Jennifer, at least all those apart from the very brave, the design outlaws with buckets of talent and their own thoughts. What intrigued me about these sessions was that it was a lighting class, but we didn't talk about the lighting: we talked about the play, and we talked about the text. We often had another play to read for another lighting class, so keeping up with the reading was sometimes tough, and you were pleased to assume the thoughtful, would-be lighting designer pose, because you did not have a clue what the dramaturgs were talking about.

Eventually the truth dawned on me that we were not going to talk about lights in this class, the reason being that *nothing exists without the text*. And without understanding the text, you cannot understand or arrive at decisions about what you are going to do with it. The doctrine was to read the play at least twice before even thinking about design.

For the lighting designer this is tough: we soon realized that you actually do not always have to read the play at all, you can just 'skim read' and take notes from the bits in italics at the beginning of every act or scene. Nevertheless, although sometimes this is possible, I would urge you to *never* do it: only the very great are allowed this privilege, and by then there are reasons why they are the very great. And also it helps to know that Fred gets killed in Act 2, which prevents you asking the director 'So where does Fred stand in Act 4?'

It is important to remain as open-minded as possible throughout all readings of the script because there is so much to learn before thinking about light.

Your response to a play or piece should not be only a technical one: you have to meet it with understanding. You are an artist, you are a designer, you are offering your response and vision of a piece, how it looks, with that design, with light. This part of the lighting designer's job is not technical: there is more to the journey. How often have you sat in the auditorium on opening night or during a final rehearsal, and the penny has dropped: 'Oh, *that's* why...!'. A little like finishing a novel and then going back to re-read the first chapter, and you find the story of the book right

Scenes from an Execution.

there in the first few pages, which when you started reading meant nothing.

Directors have the skill of understanding text, and often they are also visualizing the scenes in three dimensions for the stage. The designer, through more detailed meetings, is privy to the director's inner thoughts, and the lighting designer has to catch up to, and get to know these things also. It is great if you can have the in-depth conversation, but often the director is all talked out by the time they get to you. The lighting designer needs to be a good listener, speedy on the uptake, and quick to interpret.

So for *Execution*, despite the fact that the light plot will not be realized until the last moment, the design has nevertheless begun. After reading the play a couple of times, the parts are written out in italics at the top of each section or chapter, as are notes from the text, or a copy of the script highlighted and scribbled on. Each individual will have their own style – each to their own, it is all note-making. The bottom line here is that all scenic and visual information is extracted from the text.

EARLY THOUGHTS AND INFLUENCES

An actor lives with the text and the part. The lighting designer goes away and simply chews all the information over, thinking about it on the tube, the train, before going to sleep, quiet moments and, for a big project, thinking about it when you really should not be. Thinking about what you want it to look like. And this has nothing to do with the equipment, but what mood and location and story will be told by the lighting.

During another lighting class a discussion was thrown up about the colour of night-time after a night wash of Rosco #85 had been placed into a conceptual lighting design. Asked for a reason as to why Rosco #85, the answer given was that 'It looked good'. This failed the test, and the class was recalled for 10pm that evening, at which time we all arrived, filing past the pencil sketch portrait of Stanley McCandless (one of the American pioneers of modern stage lighting; he wrote one of the earliest classic texts *A Method of Lighting the Stage* in 1932) on the wall, and sat in the wood-panelled, bare-floored classroom. And then when all were seated, the lights were turned off and the question asked, 'What is the colour of the night?' The answer was a dull, dusty, streetlight orange, and ultimately as far removed from #85 as could be. In fact the night is never any of those deep blues; not even James McNeill Whistler, bobbing about in his boat on the Thames, found a Rosco #85 blue.

But of course this is the theatre, where we suspend belief, and we can make the night whatever colour we want. The message is not to 'never use' a deep blue for a night-time scene, but if you do, to understand exactly why. The theory can be extended to something as simple as: do not put a colour in any lamp. Unless you have a reason, a good *design* reason for doing so – and then you may!

The text is always with me, and at times the thinking does involve actual lighting instruments, but for the moment these thoughts are pushed away. Also being considered and digested is the set design, and the theatre space itself.

The set design places an object or objects in space; they have a scale, colour and texture, and they also have a story to tell. The set designer is in the hands of the lighting designer almost from the outset, and a designer who appreciates this can make provision for light in their designs. Other designers offer challenges by proposing seemingly insurmountable problems – for example, allowing less than a metre upstage in which to backlight a painted back-projection screen. A general rule, open to conjecture, could be stated as 'The more minimal the scenery, the more potent the lighting shall need to (and can) be'.

The work of Canadian director **Robert Lepage** and Ex Machina is familiar to English audiences through productions at the Almeida, the Riverside Studios, or the National Theatre. Through them it has become apparent that Lepage is a director of genius, and that he is also a master of the minimal with a sophisticated use of theatre craft. What John Pawson (architect and designer, who published a seminal book entitled *Minimal*) would say is that there is nothing unsophisticated about minimal, and then nod in the direction of Japan.

The Robert Lepage pieces often use practical light sources contained within a set – for example, an advertising duratran (a gigantic photographic image printed on a material that can be backlit to illuminate it), or a small shaving light. There may be shadow play with puppets or actors, or projection work on surfaces that move to deliver you into the next scene. Within a setting may be closely played scenes lit with a single practical. Often a scene is lit with only two or three other units, carefully placed. You don't often get the chance to work like this, and it is a method born out of much rehearsal time.

Another example of such care and close attention to detail is the work of **Michael Hulls**, and particularly alongside that of choreographer Russell Maliphant (*see* page 136). He has the benefit of not only lots of rehearsal time, but a choreographer who can be said to 'work a space', where movement is studied and confined to smaller areas of stage, and dance is created that has a careful and intricate construction. This helps Hulls, as he knows exactly where a dancer will be on stage and for precisely how long a time. His lighting design therefore, often using a single lamp in place of many, ends up with a purity of language matching that of the choreography, and is used to great effect, as their pieces testify.

THE SET

The design for *Scenes from an Execution* involved an octagonal bare, long wooden floor, stretching up- and downstage. The floor was treated so as to look like that of a painter's studio, with different colours of paint spattered and spilt all over it. There was a trap downstage centre, with the hatch opening downstage. Thus the die is instantly cast: the design is minimal, and clever, and it is clear straightaway that the lighting will have to do a lot of work.

For this production the Dundee Repertory Theatre was also converted for the first time into 'the round'; being already somewhat of the thrust/proscenium fusion, the theatre in fact lends itself to this. The seating capacity of the auditorium was also reduced to create intimacy for the space.

In addition to the stage floor, for various scenes there were other scenic elements, such as a cow carcass, a chandelier, a wooden painter's canvas frame, a gilded painting frame and a ladder. There were also to be statues for one scene, a drape on a spot line, and a platform of scaffolding. So the set design, whilst at first appearing minimal, now begins to seem quite rich.

All of this is taken on board and mulled over, for as much time as possible. There is also some 'research' to do: reading, an exhibition or two, quiet time to think, a chat about abstract things to others, thinking about previous shows designed and seen, and suitable new ones to take in – and all the while thinking about all the possibilities of how it could look, and also how to achieve this, alongside what will actually be expected. This latter is probably the most important.

Two important lessons learnt are vital here: firstly, that no matter how big or small a stage set

Scenes from an Execution.

is, when given the design, assume that a director shall want to see an actor's face anywhere on that stage – and that means anywhere, from the extreme upstage corner to the extreme downstage opposite corner. If there is a ladder involved, then you will need to light for the top of it. The design has to cater for all such eventualities.

Secondly, sometimes in a larger theatre, 35 per cent and 45 per cent levels just do not work; there is a director and an audience out there that want to see and be entertained, so accept that 70 and 80 per cent will be needed. Yes, sometimes it will feel to be too much, but you simply have to do it. In other words, where one's artistic instinct may be

The tension wire grid – a wonderful Canadian invention – not only allows the crew easy access to the equipment, but it also has a full 360° view of the theatre, ideal for a space that converts from a conventional proscenium into an in-the-round configuration. (The Vanbrugh Theatre, London.)

to create shadow and to play with chiaroscuro and intrigue, on some occasions you just simply need to make the action visible – and it is always best to be prepared for this eventuality. Even Art sometimes needs to bend to necessity.

As all these considerations are being thought through, the layering of issues to deal with is already becoming huge. They all concern the information given to work on, and the process of creating and arriving at how the piece is to look, and thus how the show is going to be lit. And yet, quite rightly, still no real thought has been given to the equipment itself.

In-the-Round

There is more information to consider. The architecture of a theatre or a space critically affects how a piece can be lit. An in-the-round theatre will have been built, hopefully with the use of a good consultant, to include the necessary lighting positions on which to rig the instruments. The bane of many a lighting designer is the thrust setting (a stage 'thrusting' into the audience from within a proscenium, i.e. allowing for audience seated on each side of a fore-stage), not because it is thrust, but because a decision is made to offer a thrust piece in a proscenium theatre – that is, use the orchestra pit to bring the action closer to the audience. What this means, in effect, is that the lighting positions, often judged on variations of the 45 degrees theory, become all wrong.

Continuity in general cover washes from the auditorium and underneath the proscenium is the norm. Of course this is not impossible, but it is sometimes difficult without the right positions, with washes often becoming slightly steeper or shallower than ideally one would like; or maybe the first two bars of the system will be fine, but the last is steeper or shallower, and vice versa. Modern theatres are now often designed to convert into several spaces and accordingly provide methods and gadgets to do this, but they are rarely totally successful!

The Dundee Rep is a proscenium, with the option of a thrust. It is not 'in-the-round', and therefore the alarm bells began to ring, because it is clear that for downstage, about a metre in from stage edge, where an actor will frolic for the whole of the show, there will be no conventional lighting positions.

THE DESIGNER'S GROUND PLAN

Set designers differ in their ability to produce ground plans and sections, though fortunately some plans can often be better than they look. And remember the written word: I once telephoned **George Izenour**, the American theatre architect of huge repute, to ask him some questions on architecture; after some minutes of chatter he said to me, 'It's all in the book'. Okay, I said, and pursued whatever topic it was, only later to be confronted with another 'It's all in the book'. And yes it is, to be fair – but it is one heck of a book! And most answers can be found in books, or if not an answer, then an opinion, at least.

Once, when working with the designer **Anthony Lamble**, I would call and ask, and he would say, 'It's all on the plan'; and so the process would continue. A Lamble plan can be a piece of paper more akin to a palimpsest of the last month of his life: you can see where he has redrawn, you can see his thoughts. When you read the distinctive text, all the information is indeed there; so it is important to make good use of this vital piece of paper.

Neil Warmington, the designer for *Scenes from an Execution*, is the first designer to deliver me plans in CAD form. There was a full set of drawings, in plan. It is rare to get a side elevation, or even a section; however, a lighting designer needs at least one section of the theatre, because from this you can produce your own. The section enables you to see the air of the theatre space, and how lighting positions and the design and the building spatially connect. Usually someone in the theatre has one. Eventually the production manager at the rep. supplied me with drawings at 1:25 and 1:100 of the whole auditorium.

Costumes

Costume designs are even harder to get, really because the costumes often evolve through the rehearsal period, with series of fittings and concessions to director's or actors' opinions and desires. So sometimes you will be lucky. However, for the design process they are crucial, even if the cast are all in black: shine the wrong shade of deep blue on to black, and it will appear maroon. This happens with other colours, and with scenery.

A student at the Central School of Speech and Drama for a production of Noel Coward's *Present Laughter* provided painted samples of what the floor marbling effect was to be like, and these were invaluable. Jon Bausor, for several dance pieces, gave me a swatch card of the actual fabrics that were to be used; Anthony Lamble provided a set of colour copies of his drawings for *Serjeant Musgrave's Dance*; Neil simply said 'All the costumes are neutral colours': sometimes this has to be enough!

So far no lights have been designed or even sketched, but all the information to do so is there. Should it all be listed, it is quite a mix to carry around in one's head. But there it is, ticking over; the occasional glance at a drawing, and the occasional thought, or maybe an idea.

Conceptual Hook-Up

Jennifer Tipton works through all ideas conceptually first. In order to understand this better you could say the lighting is listed *ideally*. From the beginning of the design process there will be drawings, maybe in colour. The drawings then evolve into light plot ideas that get listed. These ideas do not revolve around the technicalities of the theatre space to be worked in yet, only the perfect theatre space. So a list is made of everything I think will be needed to light the show, from a light bulb to a VariLite (an intelligent light – *see* page 71). This can then be listed in order of priority, the most important ideas coming first.

continued on page 96

OVERLEAF: **First Impressions.** *Neil Warmington's CAD ground plan for Dundee Rep Theatre as sent to the lighting designer. It shows the seating and stage layout. Compare with the lighting plan on pages 98–9.*

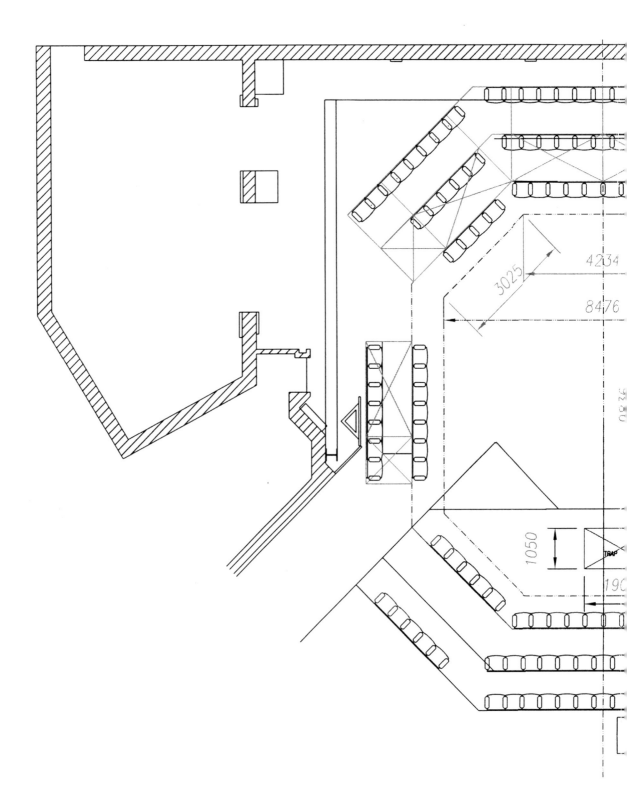

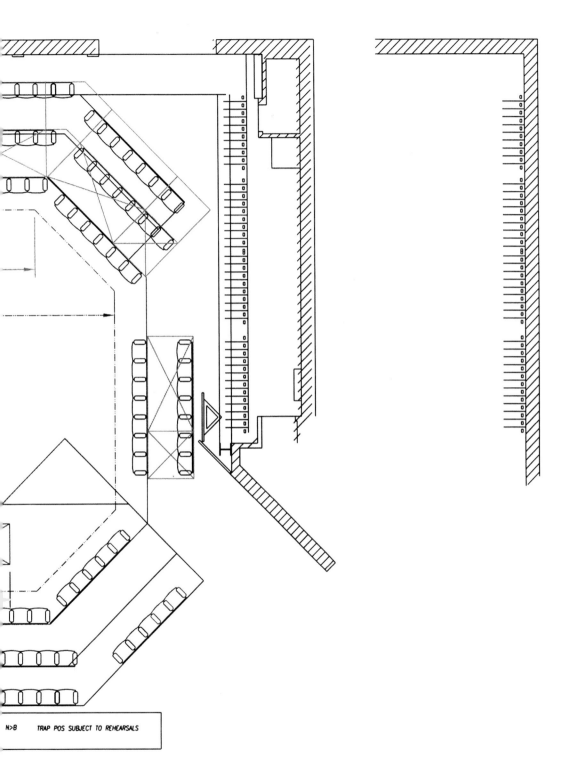

N>B   TRAP POS SUBJECT TO REHEARSALS

There will also be conceptual colour charts or lists. And then this information can be brought into a 'conceptual hook-up', 'hook-up' being an American term for a way to list instruments, and now especially linked to the Lightwrite programme. Whether software, pen or pencil are used, however, it is still *a list*.

This is therefore the order in which the decisions are made whenever I am going to light a show:

1. I arrive at a concept of what I want to do,
2. how I'm going to do it, and therefore...
3. ...what it will look like.

Rehearsals

Lighting designers use the rehearsal process in different ways. It is usually allied to the amount of free time you have. Mostly, when time is available, attendance at rehearsal is nearly always a good thing. However, there are always occasions when you catch the play only in sections and do not see the final run-through. It also depends on how the director works. Simon Usher will work a moment over and over and over. This is not interesting and we do not need to see it – boredom can also be an enemy. Simon has also asked me to leave the rehearsal room because something is not ready to be seen.

However long you stay in rehearsal, the result is the same as reading the play – that is, you have to understand the text. Understand the emotional thread of a piece, understand and empathize with what is being re-enacted, and your ideas cannot go far wrong. Sometimes, with a play about a family or politics, this is easy. With a play set in the Urals in Russia containing more abstract ideas than characters, it is not – hence the need for differing levels of research. As with all works, though, whether music or art, there is an order, and a flow of events. Lighting and sound can support and tell this story just as much as do the actors; after all, without the lights you wouldn't even see them!

So if a scene is to be played, and there is an emotional shift at a point in it, how will that shift be communicated? Just by the text; by text and lighting; or by text, lighting and sound?

The director chooses, it is part of their job, but sometimes they will also let you choose, so you absolutely need to know what story is being told. Watching rehearsals you will also develop a conceptual cue synopsis or list of cues, and have therefore the last piece of information that you require before drawing up the plan.

Drawing Up

In an ideal world the process goes as follows: the ground plan is placed on to the drawing board with a new piece of drafting paper taped on top and sections, pens, stencils and drawing things nearby. As each lighting cover or system is thought through it is drawn in, and the plan grows to completion over about two weeks. However, due to the constraints of time this hardly ever happens, and the actual drawing has to be executed in a much tighter time frame. All manner of factors determine how the plan arrives at the theatre: sometimes it is posted, though more often than not it is now, with the aid of CAD, emailed. In the past it has also been faxed.

For a plan drawn by hand, the resulting lighting always seems to be better, probably because the ideas are clearer in the mind and then on the paper. Because Neil Warmington had drawn his plans in CAD, it followed for this piece that his drawing could be used as the basis for the lighting plot. In the end the drawing was worked on for three days.

Before the plan is drawn, and depending on the equipment and positions available, you have to do angle drawings and sections in different scales to work out the throw from various distances. Naturally this affects how and where you choose to place the general cover lamps.

With the space being changed architectually to in-the-round, a new environment was being created, and the lighting had to reflect this, too. The seating arrangement of the theatre radiating out on two sides and from the centre formed the natural front and angled sides of the stage. This was then mirrored upstage, in that Neil went with the natural form of the building for his stage shape, the logical solution (*see* illustration – the ground plan, pages 94–5).

The grid overhead was to be stripped, therefore the lights forming the ceiling needed to have an order and a logic in order to be in harmony with what was happening below. Lighting rigs are often symmetrical for dance, and on this occasion, too, symmetry was to be an important aspect of the design. Out of the sketching and drawing process it became apparent that if you squared off the angles of the octagonal space you had a square, or rather a rectangle: in other words a normal stage, simply rotated through 45 degrees.

Colour Choice

The colour palette needed to go through warm to cool, and include evening. After much deliberation GAM 842 was settled on as the main general cover colour for most units, the plan being to support this with washes of L203 (1/4 CT Blue), L162 (Bastard Amber), three further increasingly dark blues, an open white wash, and a warm wash: eight washes for an in-the-round setting. (GAM, meaning the Great American Market, is a major manufacturer of colour (and gobos) and much used in the US. In the UK, Lee Lighting holds a similar place, hence L being used to prefix any of their colour range. The prefix # is used for colour made by Rosco.)

Ideally you would have eight times the GAM wash for each colour; however, due to the limitations of equipment and space, this was simply not possible, so now you have to design with the lights technically, making decisions concerning power and spread, along the lines of 'What can I do with four of these, that would take eight of another?'.

Equipment Choice and Control of the Space

It had already been decided how to carve the space with light, separate areas on the floor, and create the look of the light in the air – what the quality of the light was to be like. However, what to use? The wash from Parcans is completely different from a wash with Source 4's (an axial profile).

One factor is always certain: you need to be able to land light in the centre of the stage and, especially with an in-the-round setting, everything will radiate away from this. With control of centre,

looking at the size of the stage space and the height of where you want the lighting bars to trim, you will know whether the stage will be best to split into three areas across, or five – an odd number of areas naturally providing a centre area.

The amount of power you need from the lights shall also determine this. In the USA they often will spend time working out footcandle calculations, worrying about amount lumens and colour temperature (*see* page 33). (A footcandle is the imperial unit of illumination, based on the amount of light given by a single candle at 1ft distance on to a foot square white card; the metric equivalent is a lumen.) This is all well and good, but in British Theatre we really tend to work largely through a knowledge of simply what a light times twenty will look like, and if it is going to be bright enough to satisfy your own eye. Laziness or natural ability? You decide. If you want more precision, in TV or film the need to work to an instrument, the camera, requires just such attention to technical detail with colour temperature.

From rehearsals of *Execution* it was apparent that the director was using the space split into nine areas, and the props and furniture positions fell into one of these areas. Therefore keeping the light out of the audience's eyes and controlling the stage led me to decide on a nine-point top wash. Wanting to have control of colour then doubled the instruments.

The GAM wash was to be the workhorse wash of the design and rig, the wash to be called on to provide light in any part of the stage. G842 is a gel that falls somewhere between L202 (1/2 CT Blue) and L201 (CT Blue). Often as a designer in the UK you find yourself with the Lee swatch book saying 'Well, L201 will be too cool, and L202 not cool enough', and GAM gels sometimes fall in between. Also, the units being used for the main wash, by virtue of their quantity on the kit list, were to be Starlette/ADB 1000W fresnels. There is absolutely nothing wrong with these instruments if they have been maintained well.

continued on page 100

OVERLEAF: **The finished lighting plan for Scenes from an Execution.**

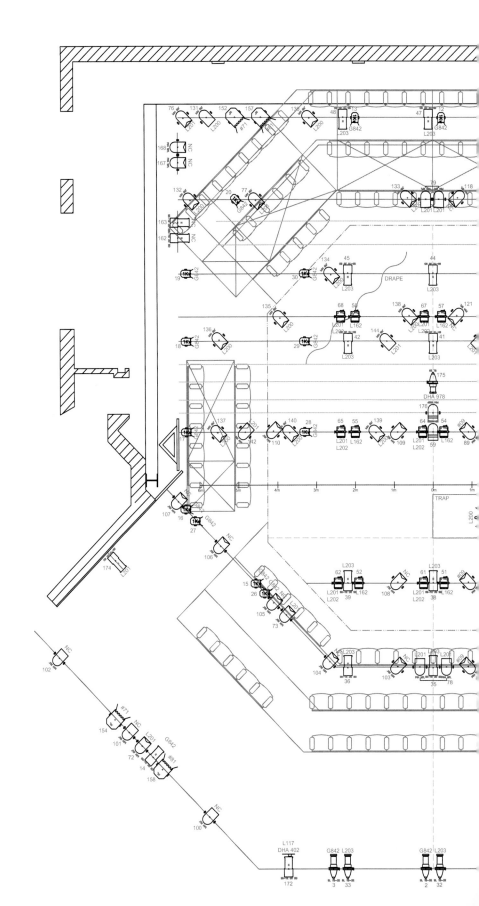

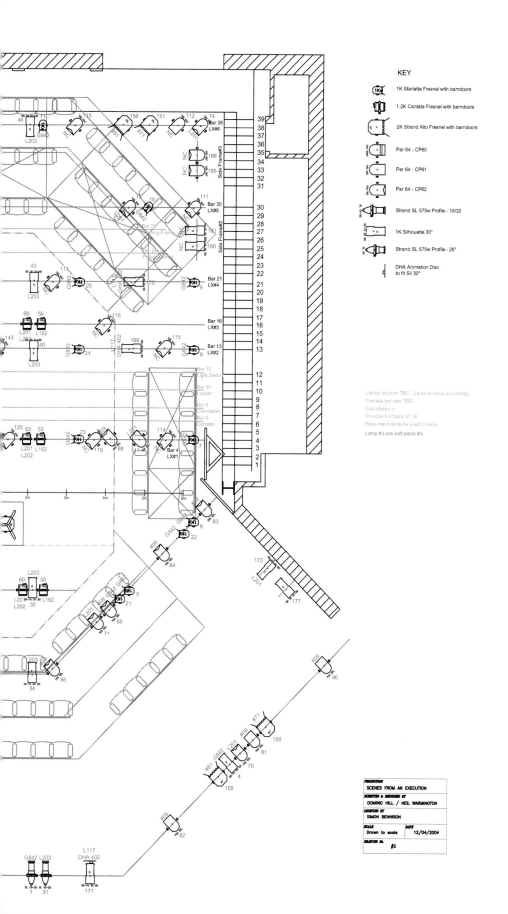

99

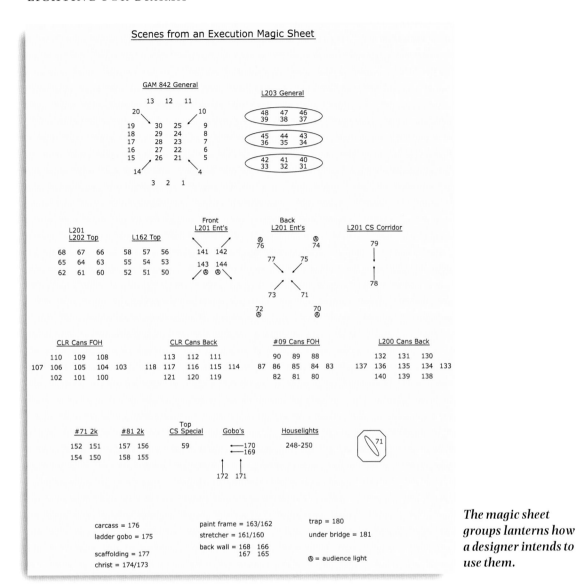

Scenes from an Execution Magic Sheet

GAM 842 General

```
        13   12   11
    20              10
  19      30   25      9
  18      29   24      8
  17      28   23      7
  16      27   22      6
  15      26   21      5
    14              4
        3    2    1
```

L203 General

```
    ( 48  47  46 )
    ( 39  38  37 )

    ( 45  44  43 )
    ( 36  35  34 )

    ( 42  41  40 )
    ( 33  32  31 )
```

L201
L202 Top
```
68  67  66
65  64  63
62  61  60
```

L162 Top
```
58  57  56
55  54  53
52  51  50
```

Front
L201 Ent's
```
141  142
143  144
  /Ⓐ  Ⓐ\
```

Back
L201 Ent's
```
 Ⓐ        Ⓐ
 76        74
   77    75
     73  71
   72        70
   Ⓐ        Ⓐ
```

L201 CS Corridor
```
     79
      ↑
      ↓
     78
```

CLR Cans FOH
```
    110  109  108
107 106  105  104  103
    102  101  100
```

CLR Cans Back
```
        113  112  111
118 117 116  115  114
        121  120  119
```

#09 Cans FOH
```
      90   89   88
87 86  85   84   83
      82   81   80
```

L200 Cans Back
```
        132  131  130
137 136 135  134  133
        140  139  138
```

#71 2k
```
152  151
154  150
```

#81 2k
```
157  156
158  155
```

Top
CS Special
```
59
```

Gobo's
```
 ←—170
 ←—169
    ↑
    ↓
172  171
```

Houselights
```
248–250
```

```
 ⬡ 71
```

carcass = 176
ladder gobo = 175

scaffolding = 177
christ = 174/173

paint frame = 163/162
stretcher = 161/160
back wall = 168 166
           167 165

trap = 180
under bridge = 181

Ⓐ = audience light

The magic sheet groups lanterns how a designer intends to use them.

However, to the modern eye, used to brighter sources – in particular the Source 4 and Strand SL unit – the light from these lamps can appear too warm and muddy. This also contributed to the colour choice.

The (mostly) fresnel units were positioned literally in a ring around the perimeter of the space to wash from their own side to the centre (*see* **channels 1–20**, on the lighting plan, pages 98–9). Then there was an inner ring to follow on the wash to the opposite side (**channels 21–30**). The peculiar aspect of an in-the-round setting, that one person's front light is someone else's backlight, means that by continuing the washes in this fashion everything is even in all directions. And the actors become lit not only when looking out, but crucially when looking in towards the centre of the space, which in effect is what they do more often. Therefore the GAM wash had to work, the design theory being once the scene is lit, then other washes and units can provide further sculpting possibilities.

The GAM wash was supported by a nine area 45° 1K Sil30 wash in L203, working up- and downstage (**channels 31–48**). In effect what the Gam could not do, the L203 would. It would add extra power, a warmer tone, and the ability to either front/backlight into an area, or side light into an area again, depending on its position to the audience.

Colour Balance

A balance in the colour palette was required, essentially the ability to operate from warm to cool. I have seen this done in the past with just OW (clear or open white) and L201, and some would argue that this is all you need.

To offer two examples: Spanish lighting designer **Nicolas Fischtel** was lighting a ballet in an open-air theatre one summer, where the production electrician had failed to organize any gel for the rig. Defiant, he opted to fight fire with fire, and said, 'Fine, I shall light it in open white.' Which he duly did, and declared the results superb. This is possible due to the eye's ability to perceive intensity and then translate that into mood, and the fact that the physical effect of the light on its own also works without gel through 0 to 100 per cent, to reveal many shades and moods. This can also be connected and referred to the Tipton theory of only using colour when you have to, and the common operatic form of lighting through OW and the Lee correction filters.

Secondly, once lighting a play for the Arcola theatre in East London, I found a collection of kit that not even Jim Laws (theatre historian, and a renowned British collector of ancient and beautiful period lighting instruments and other theatre paraphenalia) would find a home for. After half of it had been fixed, the luxury of acquiring gel frames was not an option. Deciding to go entirely colour free, the result was bizarrely very pleasing. Try it some time, it works.

Paule Constable, currently one of our best designers, has manufactured a signature look for herself through the dedicated use of OW, and then the Lee correction filters going to L200 (Double CT Blue) cool and L204 (Full CT Orange) warm. The

reasoning is flatly, 'Well, what more do you need?' And well, she is absolutely right. Her use of L200 when seen in her colour palette through the course of an evening is similar in effect to many other's use of far deeper blues.

So in effect, colour balance becomes comparative from the very start. Paule's is probably OW. For me this time it was GAM 842. This was taken a shade cooler with a top wash of L201/L202, and warmer with the second top wash in L162 (*see illustration overleaf*).

Lee market L200 as the equivalent of double L201. However, it is not. L200 becomes quite a different gel, at times looking very blue or almost lavender, edging into L137 (Special Lavender)/ L142 (Pale Violet)/#55 territory. Ideally L200 would have been in the top wash, but it felt too dark, and risky. Double L201 could be too blue, so the compromise of L201/L202 seemed a good idea, and also complemented the GAM and the L203 washes better. It is possible that L161 (Slate Blue) would have done the job also, but it could have come up too misty.

L162 is a much underrated and underused colour. Also, other gels such as L152 (Pale Gold) or #05 and #03 are equally fine for flesh tones. The L162 was used because it is very kind to skin, and would probably bring out the warm tones in the floor better. On low check it can give a lovely warmth, and in use in Cantata 1.2Ks it was this warmth at times I would be after.

Specials

Specials is a bizarre term really: a special light for a special job. Or rather – this person is sat on a chair – I need a light over there now – a special! Observing various rules about the use of specials, it is more of an art than simply having a light ready above the chair. For all these examples let us assume we are lighting the actors to be seen, rather than playing with dramatic mood.

An off-Broadway show called *Aven'U Boys*, with lighting by **Jan Croeze**, was impressive on the lighting side. There were several scenes where an actor was caught in an area on the stage lit by a 'special' that actually was a combination of many beams, possibly up to five or six units. The units were lighting from different parts of the theatre, and therefore in their beam angles offered different shades of light to their subject. The resulting architecture in the air was intriguing, because radiating out from the point on the stage were beams of light that had been 'designed' to look like that. It was impressive because it seemed to connect the action on stage like a fine spider's web to the auditorium. It looked good and communicated the play's action outwards.

David Hersey uses a similar technique by using a range of colours on one spot or scene. There could be OW, L201, L117 (Steel Blue), L442 (¼ CT Straw) in units all coming from different angles

and with a bright beamlight as a followspot, the textures and colours within the beams and angles delicious to the eye. In addition, if you are lighting a face, then place the lamp where it will do the job; a high-angled top light or one from the side will simply generate more trouble in creating unwanted shadow. Put the lamp front-of-house, and punch it in; sometimes an audience just wants to see!

Scenes from an Execution needed specials, but the play was rehearsed in bits, so the full run was very late in the process, at a time when the lighting design had already been required at the theatre. Therefore design needed built-in units available to work as specials.

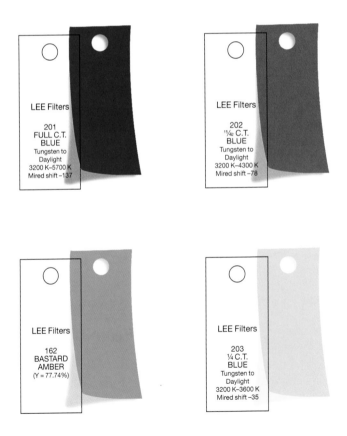

G842: general cover. L201/L202: top light #1. L162: top light #2. L203: extrageneral/slide cover. Gel manufacturers supply swatch books free of charge.

In most designs it is not unusual to pop in a couple of extra lamps as 'just in case' units. However, this can also work negatively, as who is to say that the angles they give you are what you would have designed – and yet there they are, temptingly in the rig, ready to go. But using such units could be said to dilute the purity of an overall design concept, and adding the 'spares' into a rig could also be said ultimately to show only indecision. What to do?

The general cover had been designed to be able to isolate any point on the stage, but they were also wash lamps. A last look at the kit list showed that parcans were really the only units left. Specials need to be more defined beams of light, but knowing where the lights would come into use created an opportunity to think of a potential 'wash' of specials. **Michael Hulls** occasionally uses parcans in his pieces to create washes, and an experience when designing a play called *Holes in the Skin*, for the Chichester Festival, came to mind. A pre-designed rig by **Peter Mumford** had been in place for the season. The rig had several banks of parcans, which were there for a good reason.

The idea was explored, and eventually the parcans left over were arranged into four 'systems', each system coming in at the angle of the side angles of the set floor. Ideally you would need these units hung with even spacing on diagonal bars, but since this was not possible, they were placed in positions as near as could be. The most important factor was the symmetry between the four systems – that when rigged, the spacing and look in the air had a visual harmony to it. Over the stage this

was fine for the backlight washes, but it was more difficult when moving front-of-house because the lighting positions were so different. However, there was still symmetry in the hanging of the lamps. The farthest lamps front-of-house became CP61s, and all the others CP62s.

Some time was spent deciding on the bubble size for the washes: mediums (CP61s) would work, and would offer greater scope for the lamps working as true specials, although the wide CP62s would equally be fine. With the show being in the round, these pars ultimately became multi-directional washes that could also be specials, as the idea required.

Choosing colour for these washes would also create another layer of storytelling for the piece, and just as there was a range of light to dark colouring in the washes of the main rig, the same could be done here. The choice could not be too bold, and this time L200 became a further blue after the L201/L202 combination of the top light. Balancing the other way, #09 took the warm a stage further on from the L162. There could possibly be better shades of amber, but for this design thinking of the Palace scenes and the Doge, #09 would add the required grandeur and lift. The other two directions were left Open White. For these un-gelled washes, intensity was going to provide the colour, and would allow them to mix well with the other lamps.

In the end the parcans turned out to be a very powerful idea, with the pars coming in from the four corners. The cans focused straight in, with the beam's longer axis up and down, the bubble's

Lighting colours (gels) as described in the text.

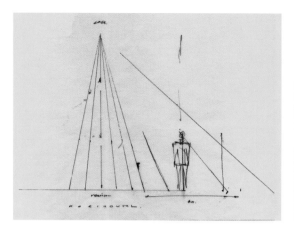 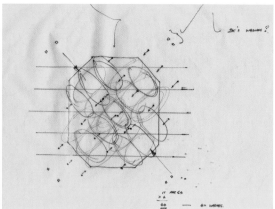

Two worksheets showing par beam angles and the arrangement of
beams across the stage.

CP62s at a trim of 6.5m. The system had three waves of three lamps one side, five across the middle, and three for the opposite side (*see* units on the plan – pages 98–9. **OW pars, channels 100–121; #09 pars, channels 80–90; L200 pars, channels 130–140**).

Forty-four pars were used in all. This is the kind of territory where design can cross over into a lot of work. But the rig created an effective ceiling over the action, balanced in either direction with enough lamps to hit the spaces as specials.

Personal Colour Choice

Every designer has their favourite gels, and they often tell a story. The fact of the matter is that now there are possibly too many to choose from. And on the artistic side you could say that the new shades can be created from existing gels and combinations. But what is also true is that gels look different and react differently from lamp to lamp, and from show to show. There is also a science to colour theory and colour mixing that can be employed. Gels go through fads and fashions, illustrated in the work of the following three designers.

What **John B. Read** creates with the following list of gels is staggering. The palette is #61, #63, #66, #70, #71 (*see* illustration opposite). In some pieces the #66 is made to look as amber as L103, through combining it with other gels and

intensity. The #61 will become warm or cool, the #70 will look blue or green, and yet sometimes one wonders how the combination of those gels would light anything. He will make L136 look lavender or pink, #78 look lavender and cool, or warm and flesh-coloured, and #71 not look green at all but extremely warm and beautiful. He is a master of colour mixing. There was also a generation created through Fred Benthem and Strand that similarly knew how to mix colour to get exactly what they wanted, to use the colour for shade and mood. (Fred Bentham – 1911–2004 – was synonymous with the creation of British lighting equipment and its use through his association with Strand Lighting.) Another leading exponent of this very British approach to lighting is **Paul Pyant**.

Peter Mumford is an innovator, who likes to stride forwards and reinvent at each opportunity. He knows exactly what to do regarding colour mixing, and is very clever with 'cyc' washes and saturated colours; he makes deep colours work in the same way that **John B. Read** makes pastels work. His work with pastels should also not be discounted: he is indeed a master colorist in the theatre.

Mark Henderson has what could be described as a more traditional gel palette to achieve results for his work. From a very varied range of shows he will have used many gels, yet he will also happily contrast OW and L201, an amber could be #09, a lavender L136, or a green L138. His choices though are based on a thorough knowledge of what shade is going to be best for the piece. When designing shows, generally over time new colours will be added, or perhaps by turn be in or out of fashion. Newer filters, such as #318 Mayan Sun, have been quickly integrated by Mark Henderson and John B. Read into their work by being very usable shades that look good in a variety of contexts.

Another thrust of the argument is that part of our vision comes from our backgrounds; we are also open to influences and really there are no rules. The person who goes to see Titian, Rubens and Turner will produce different drawings to the one who looked at Kelly, Riley and Heron; we are products of what we have seen and been told. In lighting, there are schools of thought that use colour only where necessary, and others where the use of heavy colour is the norm, with everything open to interpretation – this is the essence of design.

To add sense to all of it, William Warfel at Yale University has done a complete survey of all gels, and has even produced a programme available through GAM. The work shows scientifically, through isobar-style charts, the relationship in the colour spectrum of all gels. Thus when someone says 'this blue has got a lot of red in it', it can be checked to see if it is very near the reds in the spectrum. The results are astonishing, and to apply this science to the use of colours to combine for 'cyc' washes can be very interesting, just as the primaries red, green, blue, combined with white are meant to (and do) achieve any colour (*see* page 30). You can also do this with any other four complementary colours. His work, books and the program are well worth seeking out.

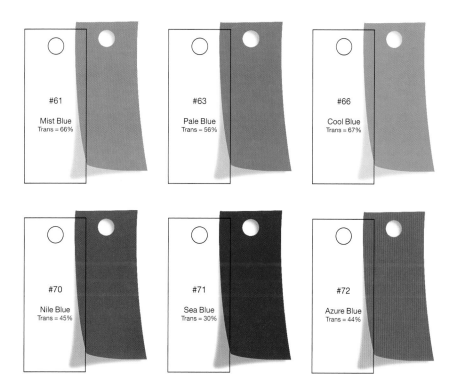

Examples of the Rosco filter Cool Blue range.

The Finished Plan

Having added and coloured the parcan washes, the design was almost complete, and (hopefully) a rig had come together of tremendous power and scope, designed to provide light over twenty scenes for an in-the-round setting. However, there were still some other lamps to add: some further up and down special pars in L201, and some lights going into the voms (vomitories: the official name for auditorium entrances and exits) to cover these specific areas. Also there were two units lighting a huge crucifix hung front-of-house; a single profile for the main actress on top of some scaffolding; and a 2K up light below the trap.

There were other last units to be put on to the plan: of the ten 2K fresnels on the stock list, one at each corner of the set was begging to be put in, and in two colours. So a wash of #81, adding a further blue beyond the L200, was included, and then a

#79	#318
Bright Blue Trans = 8%	Mayan Sun Trans = 52%
#09	LEE Filters
Pale Amber Gold Trans = 74%	138 Pale Green (Y = 79.87%)

Colours used by Read and Henderson, as described in the text on page 105.

wash of #71, which was to have two specific uses in the play – for the opening scene establishing the location as Venice, and later in the gaol scenes. For the opening scene and from the very first chat with the director and designer, Neil had asked for a wave effect to state 'Venice', and there was also a line about floating in the water. So a couple of animation discs (see page 71) with DHA402 gobos in L117 were designed in to ripple away over the bed of #71.

Other specials went into the rig for some of the scenic pieces. In addition to the hanging Christ front-of-house, there was also the painting stretcher, and the gold paint frame. Really, all these units were there to deal with elements of the set and the play that would need to be seen or made a feature of.

The plan was drawn up and annotated, bar trims (heights) were placed on it, and some rigging notes. Also included were the soft-patch numbers to add order to the rig for the lighting designer's specific use – thus the GAM wash became numbers 1 through 30, and so on. The design was sent via email for them to open and print at the theatre.

And then all that was required was to turn up and make it work!

Technical Week

A technical week is a strange beast because a schedule is produced that everybody knows will not usually be kept to; rather, it is a frame to hang the technical process around. The moral of this is that events do not always go according to plan: you have to be flexible.

It can be said (or moaned) that the lighting designer's job is the most difficult because you see the design late; you are not consulted as much as the designer; you often have to design a rig without seeing a run; and you are meant to create a worthy element to the show at the last minute, and under pressure. Of course all of this is true, but it is also just the nature of your job, and in some ways becoming good at dealing with all this is how one becomes successful. An important part of these trials and rituals is the need to remain positive, because quite apart from anything else, no one wants to be around a negative person.

Rig and Focus

In the theatre you are in the hands of the chief electrician. This particular species comes in all shapes and sizes, and basically you need someone who sees your vision and respects you, and someone who is willing to do all the niggly jobs that make the difference.

If you have followed all steps of the design process until now, and you know exactly why the lanterns are on the plan and their purpose, then you can relax and have a great time bringing it all together. If not, then at stages along the technical week you will have questions and insecurities in your mind, doubting whether the focus will work, whether the colour will work, or questions along the lines of 'What am I going to do for this scene?', and so on.

For *Execution*, on the second visit to the theatre, problems appeared concerning finding a way to achieve the top light positions, and securing the pipe on centre. Some bargaining had to be done between departments, and the centre bar was secured. For downstage, the production manager John Miller and the chief electrician agreed between them to use some of the ceiling strutting to add an extra front-of-house advance position. With these positions in place from the sections and beam angles, the focus was going to work.

The other peculiarity that always seems to happen is that a set looks smaller in real life. However, this brings great relief after poring over the plans, because you then know that the angles and kit will work after all.

Thus the show gets hung, and hopefully coloured too. The tallescope wheels in, and the shop floor is handed over to you. There are two things learnt about a focusing session, and one is from the world of sound recording. It follows that in the recording studio the band is there, the mikes are set up, the tape is rolling, and at some point the sound engineer will offer the phrase of wisdom, 'It's all right, we'll fix it in the mix' – meaning it's not quite right, but we can look at it more closely and make it sound better later. While this kind of expression comes from experience, nevertheless the fact remains that if, when you get to the mix, you find that the raw material – what is on the tape – is not good enough, then at that point there is nothing easy you can do to remedy things.

The other lesson came when on tour with the Royal Ballet in Japan; the first date was Yokohama, the show was *Swan Lake*, and the lighting designer John B. Read. Believing he might want me to focus the rig, I had pored for hours over the plan and symbols, and though I knew in theory what John wanted, when the question was asked, 'John, do you want to focus?' and he said 'Yes', the relief was enormous. Afterwards he said to me, 'Focusing is easy; what you've got to remember is just to get the light doing the job it's meant to do, in the position it's meant to be in' – meaning, do not make it into a science, do not overcomplicate, if the focus note says 'Downstage left', then get it in there, and move on.

Both of these points should stand you in good stead, because the reality is somewhere between the two. And when focusing a rig you have to choose what lamp is part of a wash and 'will do' even though less than perfect, and which lamps need to be paid proper attention. The further fact is that once you get into plotting, technicals and rehearsals, time compresses, and what you let go, you cannot fix in the mix! Therefore you have to remember to get everything as correct as possible, because a focusing session is the only time in the process that is your time. Afterwards you play catch-up.

PLOTTING

> 'Okay, let's create a bit of history!'
> John B. Read plotting *Swan Lake*
> in Boston 2001.

There is a wonderful and scary moment for everyone's first lighting design: it occurs when all the focusing is complete and the stage is prepared for the top of the show. The production desk is out, the 'coms' are plugged in, and you sit with the plan and notes ready, the DSM on one side and the director on the other, or close by. Everyone settles, and the plotting session is about to begin. And silence... and you realize that everyone is waiting for you! At least when focusing you are just with the electricians: now you are in control of the whole theatre! You clear you thoughts again, and usually say something along the lines of, 'Okay, let's put a little something in for a pre-set.' After a while you can say, 'That'll be cue 1, time of 5 seconds.' And you are on your way.

Asked to relight Ben Stevenson's *Cinderella* for John B. Read at the Opera House in Helsinki. John gave me all the information, but one of the best pieces of advice he gave was when he said: 'Remember you have to know your cues, the choreography, and what's happening next, because it'll be *you* that drives the technical, it is down to you to push everything along and then let the stage manager know exactly what is happening.'

There are different techniques also to numbering your cues. If it is a long piece, an opera or a ballet, sometimes it helps to put Act 1 cues in the 100 cue numbers, and Act 2 in the 200s, and so on. James F. Ingalls, the American designer, when lighting *Platee* for the Royal Opera in Edinburgh 1996, used odd numbers; so he started at 1 then 3, 5, 7 and so on. This left him an even number if he wanted to insert another cue. After doing numerous dance pieces with Johanna Adams, stage manager for the Royal Ballet, we once got in a pickle over what was the first cue in the show. My Q1 would be the pre-set, hers would be the first cue of the piece. I now feel this latter method is the correct way to play it. So my pre-set will be Q0.5, and the blackout Q0.7 and the first cue of the show can become Q1 for all concerned. Of course there are many exceptions to any rule.

Plotting in the 'Tech'

There should be a plotting session. In recent years this session can waiver, owing to several factors: impossible schedules; the set build over-running; the focus session overrunning. When this does happen the decision can be made to light over the technical. If you work quickly, this technique is fine, but you have to remember to fix things along the way, because if the snag list becomes too long then the show will not be what you hoped for.

This way of working is similar to a system experienced with Chris Parry on *Search and Destroy* at the Yale Repertory Theatre in New Haven. Here, with no plotting session, a full-scale technical commenced, with everyone connected with the show present. The military scale of the operation was amazing, with headsets aplenty. What was really impressive was that at any stage of the operation, if there was a problem in any department, whether costume, sound, stage, acting, painting or lighting, everything stopped while it was fixed. So the technical/plot took days, but once done the show was run in dress form and it was already a complete show. Afterwards there would also be a full critique and notes session in the auditorium, with everyone present. This method works well, and allows for pockets of time within all the other snagging to get the lighting right.

Another example would be a technical week on the opera *Arianna* at the Royal Opera with **Alan Burrett** lighting. He eschewed a lighting session for simply lighting over the rehearsals, which was a looser approach, but it worked for him, and the show looked good.

Suffice to say, for *Execution* we also lost the plotting session time and the show was lit over the technical rehearsals. Because of good notes, this was fine, and owing to the soft-patch numbers, lights could be called with confidence.

Show Structure

It is important to get a sense of the journey of looks and moods within the scope of the play; and you should try to match your lighting to the emotional meter of the play. This goes beyond questions concerned with whether it is night or day, and is linked to what Jennifer Tipton calls the inner rhythm of a piece – the subtext, the story within the story, what we are trying to say with our lights when we fix the levels for Scene 1 to be brighter than Scene 3, and then later in Act 2 when it will be darker.

Scenes from an Execution consists of twenty scenes, some short and all important, and many linked by live scene changes. A device was used to move in and out of scenes; one employed previously on *Sea of Troubles* for English National Ballet, and *Holes in the Skin* for Chichester Festival Theatre, was to use the top light on a low check. This will have been used many times, and effectively creates a format for the plotting structure of a piece.

In Act 1 the character of the Narrator links the scenes, and he had to be lit during the scene changes. This fortunately did not need to be exact, and when the pars were used on low check the light had the right atmosphere, with the nature of the par bulb light giving a brushstroke of light over where the Narrator was, or where the easel was going to. When all was set, the lights could come up on the scene.

Scenes

The challenge of *Scenes from an Execution* comes in Act 2 when it becomes evident that the play was written for radio! There are many references to the light, whether for the quality of the light for painting, or in particular the lack of it for the gaol scenes. With such passionate exclamations about 'no light', it makes the audience aware of what they are watching, and just whether there is enough light. It is important not to let an audience worry at all (about the lighting, that is) when watching a play; you have to allow them to watch a play unfold before them with no distractions. When the mind starts to wander, that is when the throat clearing and coughing begins.

For the gaol scenes in rehearsal the director Dominic had plotted in moments to turn the lights on and off in the room, and his vision was to try and play the scenes in complete blackout. This, being a gutsy move, was one accepted at first, and frankly how often does one get to sit back and watch a scene in blackout? It makes the job easy.

However, after watching it twice in the theatre, doubts began to grow: minds were wandering and, despite there being only voices, it was hard to listen. Anxiety forced a chat with the director; it was expressed that with an audience who had come to look at something it is dangerous to make them look at nothing – especially for three scenes. There was also a danger in the fact that an audience is programmed to accept a blackout as meaning either the end of a scene or the end of a play, and even when you are successful at training them to accept scenes played in blackout, how will they know which is the final blackout of the play?

The decision was therefore made to plot in the #71 at around 7 per cent – from a distance the light was wonderfully grey, and almost non-existent. This light faded up over twenty seconds for the scene, and over this time played with the human eye struggling anyway to find something to see. With just enough light to pick out shapes of people the scene could be played and believed to be a gaol in darkness. Attention was retained and the scenes were a success, the continuity of the piece remained in place, and the audience knew when the final blackout came that it was the end of the play.

Lighting the Theatre

As the Dundee Rep changed its layout to an in-the-round space, stripping back all the masking, everything was exposed and this provided the opportunity to light the structure of the theatre itself. Pars were used to glance across the back wall, specials were used to highlight the cross, and lamps put on the underside of the lighting bridge. Together with some light haze and incense, an environment was created that was a little like walking into a church – and the stage was set.

The house lights came out of lamps eventually not used in the rig. These turned out to be all the lamps specified as entrance and exit lights for the voms. They were not needed because when an actor entered, it was a little like stepping into the ring or arena: basic, powerful theatre, with the space charged in such a way that there was no need to light the entrances and exits.

The run of *Scenes from an Execution* was an artistically successful revival for the Dundee Repertory Theatre, with good reviews. This was confirmed later in the year when both the set and lighting design were nominated in the 'Best Design' category for the Scottish Theatre Critics Awards.

THE PRICE BY ARTHUR MILLER
FOR THE TRICYCLE THEATRE COMPANY

Scenes from an Execution was an example of an adapted piece in a rearranged theatre space. *The Price* serves as a study on lighting the 'normal' play. It is a neglected play by Miller from 1968, which, owing to muted though not unfavourable response, and the higher profile of his other plays, has led to it not being often performed in Britain. Nicholas Kent from the Tricycle Theatre had the courage to go out and assemble a top-notch cast in Warren Mitchell, Sian Thomas, Larry Lamb and Des McAleer. He then asked Sean Holmes to direct, and brought along designer Anthony Lamble and myself for the lights – and gave us all the challenge of producing a worthy revival.

The show opened in October 2002, and the design was worked on over Easter and through the summer of that year. Anthony asked me along to a pre-design meeting at his studio, before the meeting with the director, so I knew there must be a substantial design problem to solve; and when I saw the set, sure enough, there it was: a roof and a skylight. And then the question, 'Do you think it will be a problem?'

It is superb for the lighting designer to be included right at the outset of a design. I have had meetings where this situation can follow two routes: there is the designer who is sometimes not clear about their final design, and picks your brain to arrive at better decisions for themselves; and there is the designer who knows exactly what they want, but they also know that to achieve it will be extremely difficult. Anthony belongs to the latter, and is very considerate and understanding of suggestions.

Put on the spot in a meeting you have suggestions, and ideas are bounced around. The tendency can be to leap into a lighting design/technician mode as you think of instant ways to light things. Sometimes you can end up reaching hasty decisions, so it is good to remain diplomatic. Base the majority of decisions on what is good for the show, and not just for the lighting. Often a design/director team can present you with special effects to create. As a lighting designer this is an area where you are often on the edge of your authority and expertise; that is, we visually receive all manner of special effects through all media, and sometimes requests can be unrealistic. There are also specialists to deal with the gadget end of the business. That said, you do need knowledge of effects, and you need to know what will work and what will not. For the purposes of a meeting, you must be honest and say if an idea is not going to be effective; this ends up being positive, rather than negative information.

However, this was not a meeting of effects – it was about a skylight. With a large skylight it is logical to regard it as a source of light to be used to simulate daylight for the room. With these first thoughts Anthony was persuaded in that direction, and by the end of the meeting, he changed the position and shape of the window to accommodate lighting ideas.

A side effect of such sessions is you end up with strong lighting elements for a piece of work you have as yet not really had time to work on. These visual ideas are defined at the beginning, and instantly lead the way forwards; with no careful thought process, you are suddenly lighting a show. This is not necessarily a negative thing, as long as you take care, after the initial rush, to think things through.

It is an aspect of set design that when a design is handed in, that is the way the show will look, and generally speaking a designer cannot go back and change the colour of a backcloth, for instance. In this respect the lighting designer should think carefully before criticizing the last-minute nature of producing a plot and schedule in the theatre, because it is within those constraints that you have the longest amount of time to arrive at your design decisions, and to revise them.

The Price is set in New York. The location is the top floor of a brownstone building in a once salubrious part of town where the two brothers in the play used to live. Their father, a once successful

Photos from the 2002 production of The Price.

businessman, suffered terrible financial losses, as many did, from the Wall Street crash. In piloting survival after this tragedy, the two brothers, who had been studying science together, went their separate ways, one into medicine and the other into the police force. Eventually, after their parents die, the belongings from the pre-crash era end up on the top floor of the house, gathering dust; until, that is, Victor, the policeman, decides to sell everything to raise money.

We meet Victor at the top of the play after he has climbed the stairs to enter the apartment once again. He is looking around the apartment, examining his old belongings and once familiar objects. He is waiting for the appraiser to arrive and give him 'a price'. He has also tried in vain to contact his brother in order that he can consult with him and share the profit. Eventually, of course, the brother turns up.

The downstage set opening framed the view directly into the lounge. The walls were slightly angled to follow a perspective, and created a vanishing point upstage through the space. Two small windows on either side of centre looked out on to the brick wall of the adjacent building. The main entrance door was downstage left, the door to the bedroom mid-stage right, facing the audience. This door offset the architecture of the space, but you did not notice it because of the angled walls and vanishing point. The skylight was large and dominated the space overhead, set into the ceiling piece downstage.

For this piece, despite the design process used for *Scenes from an Execution*, my thoughts and the direction of the design were to follow two paths. The first was how to light a play with the ceiling overhead; the other was how much of a role the window was going to play. Overall, the challenge was to conjure the atmosphere for this room, in the late sixties, in New York, piled high with old and grand furniture. With these issues present, yet shoved to one side in my mind, the rehearsal and design process commenced.

The Tricycle is a wonderful place to work: a kind, small, intimate space, with a lot of history, and subject of a recent second major renovation. In its first, in the seventies, the auditorium was redesigned to create a court theatre of painted red scaffolding and canvas panels. The main lighting positions are similarly red, and formed of truss goalposts at even intervals along the ceiling space until the old proscenium of the original theatre, where it turns into a more traditional, painted, black barrel-style studio theatre grid.

Furnished with a plan and section of the space, I also had the set drawings, and some colour samples for the walls. I remarked previously on the high information content in an Anthony Lamble plan, and this model showed similar detail. It is important to realize when viewing a model that everything is there for a reason. In *The Price* design, the perspective of the set was very clever for doing two things: opening out into the auditorium to bring the actors closer, and simultaneously directing the eye through the apartment space to the room/kitchenette upstage and the window beyond.

In the model was to be read much detail: how the furniture was piled up against the walls; the colours of the walls, and where on them the plaster had come away in parts; the dust and the shading towards the corners of the set; the height of the dado rails, and the ventilation ducts over the doorway. There was wallpaper in the hallways. Also the patination of the parquet floor, and how it had been worn away through years of walking over the same area. The angle of the sofa and chair; the colour of the small curtain in the kitchenette, and the marble bust in front of the sink; the detailing and colour of the ceilings. All these details were surely there for good reasons, and elements Anthony would expect to see.

An important aspect of lighting is that sometimes it is just as much what you do not light, as what you do. A corner painted dark and shaded is sometimes meant to be just that, and should be handled carefully. As **Paule Constable** would tell you working with designer John Macfarlane, the surrounding dark almost plays an equal role. Another potential trap, which always lies ready to strike at any time, is that you do not necessarily have to light a colour on the set with a similar

*Early version of the
set model during
design meetings.*

colour in the light. If a floor is brown or a curtain is red, you do not need to make them look anything other than what they are: the colour is there already.

So for this design I had to take a step back from the detail, and concentrate not on the scenery, but purely on the figures. That is, I knew to an extent the detail would take care of itself. In fact, with scenery so complete, my job became one of not making any dramatic lighting gestures: I had to make sure the actor would look good within the set, and support the journey of the text.

THE DESIGN PROCESS

The action of the play begins in the late afternoon at the end of a working day in the city, and then continues in real time through the course of the play. So, as there is a journey through the story, there is likewise the journey into early evening in the apartment, and the space would have to reflect the change in atmosphere in the room from the changing light outside.

The design process began in exactly the same way as always: reading the script twice, and so on.

There was the benefit of chatting and meetings with Anthony; I also had a colour sample card of the wall colours, and the internet became a research tool. I punched in 'The Price' and 'Miller', and came up with the original *New York Times* reviews from the opening night on Broadway. They were interesting because the play had not been a roaring success; mentally the bar raised itself because I then knew the play was not necessarily going to run itself. We would have to work hard to make it a success.

To this day there has not been a conversation with Anthony regarding Edward Hopper. Whatever the critics write about this artist, his paintings do capture moods of the mid-twentieth-century American city, and especially interiors. The percentage of this idea in the overall look of the show was not high, but it seemed a good guide for a sense of austerity, or image that the piece seemed to require, and the set to strive for – a way to let it breathe within time and location.

continued on page 116

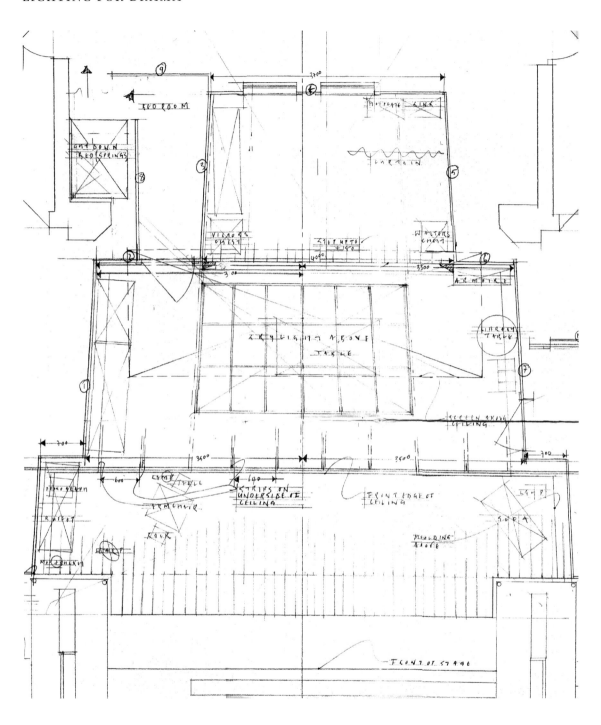

Anthony Lamble's ground plan for The Price *at the Tricycle.*

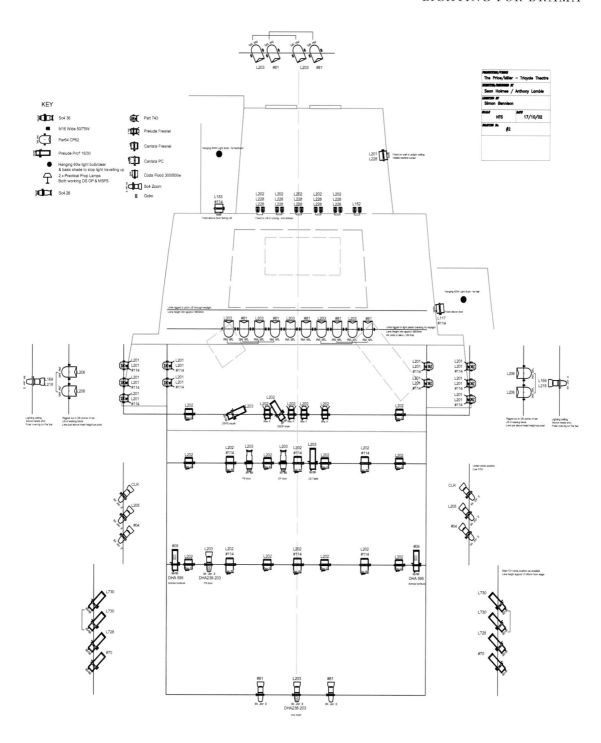

The lighting design plan for The Price *at the Tricycle.*

Angle and Shade

Colour test sheets were made to establish a palette, passage of time and the colours contained within the set. This can be as elaborate as one desires; however, it is really just a simple exercise, another stage of the decision making. It is easy when looking at the colour swatch book to be blinded by the range of possibilities on offer. By creating another range of colour samples, you can go to a reduced set of colours in the swatch, and find combinations more easily.

The skylight seemed a possible light source, and indeed it would in reality have been the main light source in the room. However, there were technical difficulties: there was to be a small back projection screen angled above the window, which was intended to be lit as a background seen through the window. Its proximity to the set meant there would not be the physical distance to use the window as a light source. Also, the properties of the plexiglass used in the window meant that to shine any light directly on to it from above would result in a reflection going back on to the ceiling of the theatre, or in fact the BP screen!

Looked at like this, the window was not going to be a workable light source at all. The BP could be lit to give the impression of late afternoon passing into evening, and thus give the appearance at least of a light source. If only we were doing the play in Prague or Berlin, and sailing in a more expressionist wind; in opera you would probably do this, hopefully, in a theatre with a fly tower! Had the piece not had A-list actors appearing in it, the risk-taking could have been higher. More than anything, the limitation here was the physical space of the Tricycle, and honouring Anthony's idea of the plastic backing screen.

With this road exhausted, it meant all other light had to come from front-of-house. What I really wanted to do here was very simply have one perfect front-of-house position hung with a three-colour wash of 2K fresnels, soft and washing straight into the set, the three colours being able to control the changing shade of daylight. This kind of idea is the essence of conceptual design: you know what you want, but how can it be achieved with the available kit?

Designing the Front-of-House Wash

There are very few theatres with perfect lighting positions; most are given to you with architect's ideas and engineer's problem solving realized – and not always helpfully! However, without vast differences in theatre structures, the lighting designer's job would be far less interesting. As we have already discussed (*see* page 92), in designing a thrust stage the set designer brings the actors closer to the audience, but for a lighting designer all the rigging positions move 1–2m from their ideal place. The result can be a front-of-house cover that is either too shallow or too steep, and connecting the angle of the washes from the front bars with the first stage overhead bars can be tricky.

Theatres with a studio-style grid are not as affected by this as are the older proscenium theatres. At a space like 'The Place' in London – a famous dance venue – lanterns can be positioned almost anywhere. The old BBC Riverside Studios in Hammersmith solves the problem with all their overhead bars able to move up- or downstage into any position.

The Tricycle is very good, with its series of structural goalpost trusses. On this occasion the set came all the way downstage to its normal position. The ceiling piece stopped with just enough space to enable a lighting position, allowing the wash to continue upstage. So, in a way, the potential problem of having a ceiling was at least compensated for by having ideal positions for the washes.

An essential concept with lighting is that the light not only makes things visible, it also creates an environment to the senses: light has physical properties in space not only for the eye, but also for the body. The concept of the single FOH bar seemed possibly too good to be true. If we were in Prague or Berlin, the walls of the set would probably be smooth, and such straight architectural lines then allow for direct thought and solutions. Straight lines from the lighting suit the manner of the production and the eye.

With the detail and clutter of *The Price* set, this approach would be too simplistic, and the physical effect of the light would be literally to push the actors into it and flatten them in the space, and to the eye. To avoid this effect, the main wash would function against this and be designed using more of the 45-degree approach, not only because it provides an effective tried and trusted method of generating a general cover (*see* page 53), but also because the angle and line of the light would get into the detail of the set better, and be sympathetic to its architecture. It would also generate a better line in the air of the theatre space, and, most importantly, it would mould the bodies, faces and costumes of the actors well. So the most important lamps of the design, the angled L202 wash in three waves, were the first lanterns to be drawn into the design.

Charles Edwards, a set designer who is so visually strong that he courageously works as a lighting designer too, recently lit a new production of *Werther* by Massenet for the Royal Opera. The initial lighting rig was not huge or complicated by any standards, but it was peppered with ideas that would or would not work. This is not a criticism, as the ideas themselves were thought through; they just did not find a role in the final design, in the 'look' of the piece. Eventually the rig was scaled down to very important lamps for scenes needing a precise focus, and the design became a powerful minimal set of instruments.

The L202, undertaking the 'pack horse' work of the evening and used throughout, also needed help, and the colour itself needed to be contrasted and balanced. Looking at the original design, this is where the L201 wash slotted in, and the Clear (CLR) and L205 units. These instruments provided colour balance, and were also quick solutions to providing 'look' changes – with two lamps crossed over and pushing into the set, it would make a quick wash in a different colour.

There were further colour washes placed into the rig to provide for transitions and colour for the set walls. Shades of steel green were picked to accent the walls as required, and a double L201 wash worked with a deeper #80 blue. There was also a wash of #66, which, as a light steel blue, acts differently at level, and also includes a degree of red in its make-up, making it kinder on skin.

Dressing the Set and Specials

The general cover divided the stage into nine areas to give flexibility for accenting the action. To define areas even further, a minimum of one special on each piece of furniture was included. The shade picked was L203, a step lighter in blue colour correction for contrast. These lamps would work on their own, or be part of a general state. Units were thus placed to light the chaise, the chair and the table, with one lamp for each doorway.

After all the thought concerning the skylight, it needed to feature in the design in some way. With no light options through the window, gobos suggestive of light through them could approximate the effect. Two gobos were therefore installed, again both from front-of-house: one was focused straight underneath the skylight to project an image as if the light were coming from above; the second was focused to wash across the chaise and stage left wall and doorway.

These units were placed after watching rehearsals and noting the atmosphere and pace of the opening moments of the play. Between curtain up and the first line there was a space: in this time the audience is waiting, and I saw an opportunity here to make enough of a visual statement to enable the patience of the audience to last over the opening silence of Victor entering the apartment he has not been into for sixteen years, looking around familiar objects, and playing an old 78 record. The gobos were placed in as an idea to create a cue sequence illustrating the passage of time through the day, moving the light around the room to get to the point in time where Victor enters the room.

Just as by overlooking points of the stage for creating a general cover system, you can often run into problems by not accounting for what 'may be needed', and in particular regarding the set. So far all the light designed has been to hit the stage, covering the actors, washing the walls. But what about the ceiling, the room upstage, the windows upstage? The remaining units in the design dealt with these questions.

There were two units placed to light the main ceiling. The upstage ceiling was lit by a flood unit fixed to the set wall upstage left of the small curtain in the kitchenette. The curtain itself was lit with a pair of M16 units. The upstage space was dealt with by a row of M16s along the upstage of the coving for the room.

The two external windows had small scenic walls built beyond them that required lighting and provided the opportunity to be lit through, giving interest to the set and props upstage. A vertical boom was positioned upstage left, with small fresnels rigged to focus through these windows in two colours. And floods were positioned on the floor to light the brick-wall backing-flat in the same colours.

The only other areas of the set to be addressed were the corridors off-stage of the doorways. A flood over each door inside the hallway at low level provided the ambient light, and a bare, clear light bulb connected to an old brass fitting hung slightly in view. The stage-left bulb was lit throughout, and the stage-right bulb turned on, on cue, in the first act.

PLOTTING THE SHOW

It is easy when reading a play as a lighting designer to be over-ambitious about the number of cues needed within a scene or over a sequence. Generally speaking, the lights should not interfere with the pace and flow of the text, or with what the director is trying to achieve: the lights are merely a device to link and support scenes. Director Sean Holmes was keen that when the curtain went up we saw the room for the play. With the bric-a-brac and furniture there is much for the eye to digest in the opening moments. He also wanted Victor to be seen as soon as he entered the room.

For the opening sequence there was also the mini story to be told concerning where we were on this day as Victor entered: the house lights faded, the special on the broken-down leather chair faded up with the street noise, just as the auditorium touched complete blackout. We certainly did not want attention to be lost or to drift at any point. The chair is an icon of the show, being the place where the spiritually broken father used to sit after the financial crash. It is also used by Solomon at the end, and almost constitutes a fifth character at times, embodying the presence of the father.

The chair special was the prompt to bring light into the room, the imaginary source being the skylight. At this point the L201/L201 in the fresnels began to fade in as an ambient light underneath a prominent first window gobo, focused straight in from front-of-house to give the impression of light entering the room from above.

The next cue took out the first gobo and brought in the second, which was focused across the chaise and stage-left wall and doorway. At this point all the light in the room and beyond the windows for outside was fading up to level. The second gobo then faded out as the room lights arrived at their first state of the show; and Victor entered.

The look was not intended to be too bright, because we are seeing the room for the first time as Victor does. It is a shadowy, New York late afternoon, and the lights are off. Also, later in the piece, I knew the lights would need to be brighter, so I needed to keep lantern level in reserve. The opening state did become brighter after Victor's preamble around the objects of the room caused him to walk into the shadows. The flexibility of the general cover meant that an area could be lifted in order to solve the problem, and fix the cue.

Once into the piece the lights acted to support the flow of the play. There was a build to anticipate Solomon's entrance. When he went to inspect the bedroom, the light bulb in the upstage right corridor came on. Act 2 began where Act 1 ended, therefore the lighting remained the same. At this point the play begins its journey towards early evening, so a series of cues were placed to maintain the level of light appropriately within the room, but for the external light to travel from cool to night. Some of these fades were 18min long, the effect being that you did not notice, as you were too caught up in the unfolding drama.

Pre-heating

In the opening cues there are a lot of lights all fading up at the same time. When the states were plotted and run in sequence, they looked dreadful until pre-heated (see page 82). With some care given to this, the lights could follow on in the cues, and the fades looked smooth.

THE PRICE TRANSFERRED TO THE APOLLO THEATRE, WEST END

The news came through that *The Price* was to transfer to the West End, and the show needed to be redesigned for the Apollo Theatre, a classic Victorian proscenium space with very different lighting positions to the Tricycle Theatre. The plan from the producers was to let it play for two more weeks at the Tricycle as a means of extended rehearsal, and then slot the show swiftly into the Apollo for an initial eight-week run.

Over the course of the original production week details in the design had changed, to make the show work in the space that would have to be updated into the new rig plan; thus:

• FOH L205 units were not used.
• The Gobo colour changed from L202 to L203.
• L730, L735, #70 wall wash units were moved to a low FOH position.
• DHA 595 gobos were pulled (ie removed) and the units re-pointed as corner room specials, in L201.
• Two units were rigged as downstage pipe ends, in L201.
• Most specials were focused hard, with frost added.
• Two units called for lighting the ceiling colour changed and became a single unit from centre-low FOH.
• L206 low side-pars were cut and replaced with minuettes, with L129 frost.
• Extra floods were placed in as floor units to light the rear brick wall backing flat.

While the rig had to be redrawn to accommodate such changes, there was also the physical change of the theatre space to consider. The stage of the Apollo happened to be almost exactly the same size as the Tricycle, or rather the set design footprint. It was as if a new theatre space had been built around *The Price* set, arriving at a space of Apollo proportions. In others words, it was a perfect fit.

The auditorium, however, was very different, transferring from a court theatre-style space into a proscenium. Where at the Tricycle there were three goalposts, the Apollo has three tiers. A deficiency of many theatre plans is that the lighting positions are rarely all drawn, especially when in an old space; positions also may have changed or altered. A visit to the theatre is essential and should be encouraged wherever possible, and copious notes made in whatever way possible: drawings, photographs, video, digital photographs.

Of the three tiers at the Apollo, on the first circle there is a small centre rail position. The second tier is a longer circle rail running two thirds of the arc. And on the top tier there are two shorter rails that continue round to the edge of the tier from where the rail on the first tier finishes. At second tier height there were two single upright bars about 3m high, and close to the second boxes. There is also the statutory proscenium boom. The stage had a full grid of fly bars, and there was a gantry cross-over between fly floors.

During a college exercise based on *The Front Page* at the Goodman Theatre, Chicago, using a similar box-style set, students bemoaned the lack of lighting positions. The advice from Jennifer was, 'As a designer it is your job to place the lights where you need them in the space, and the production electrician's job to make it happen.' Jaws dropped. It is an example of the distinct roles that exist between the technician and the designer in America. Whether this is true or not, in fiction or reality, what believing a statement like that really does is to serve as a device, just as the conceptual hook-up does, for a designer to say 'Well, really I want my lights there.' Once as a designer you are certain of this, you then psychologically know how to modify the lighting position if it is not achievable. It is a means of making good decisions without knowing you are doing it.

With the ground plan and elevation of the theatre, I set about the task of redesigning the show. I looked at the front-of-house positions and scratched my head at the lack of logic, until it was *continued on page 121*

continued on page 121

OVERLEAF: **The lighting design plan for The Price at the Apollo.**

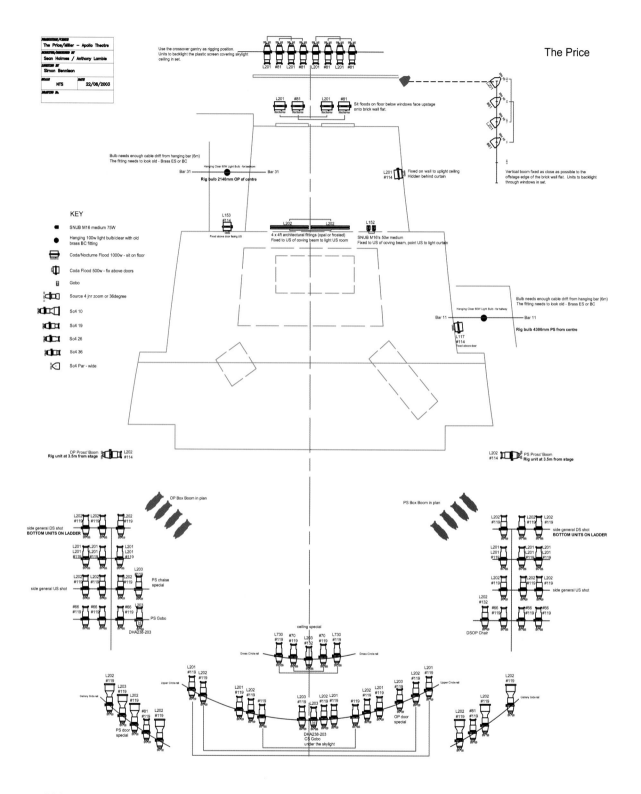

The Price

explained to me that the bar on the top tier used to be continuous until projectors were needed – at which point the centre section was taken down to the second tier. Since neither position was long enough for a full run of units, it presented the perennial problem of one bar being too flat, and the other too steep.

The original washes were made up with fresnels, but this needed to change to profiles, and exclusively the ETC Source 4 lamp. At this point you need to use and trust angles, and in particular beam landings. The second tier was saying I could use 19-degree units, and the third tier 10-degree units; and dependent on the throw from downstage to upstage, the ladder position became a combination of 19-degree and 26-degree angles.

The single box-boom bar at first seemed too small, but by out-rigging 1m arms on either side, potentially six rows of four units became a possibility, which would be enough to provide the systems required and the specials. Once the issue of where exactly the units were going to hang had been solved, then I could proceed and place the lamps on the plan. Fixtures and ideas were all consistent from the original design, apart from the coving run of M16s, which changed to four architectural tungsten strips with L202 and frost; and the low side minuettes, which became Source 4 36-degree Juniors and were rigged high on the FOH proscenium room.

Soft-patching

Whenever possible it is a good idea to soft-patch the numbers on a lighting rig (soft-patching is to allocate the channel numbers you want units to be – the lighting board translates these to the required dimmers; thus you can use any number for any unit). It allows clarity of thought and enables you to organize ideas. It transfers all the work done at the conceptual stage. However, the original production was not soft-patched and the Apollo schedule became so tight there was a need to start with cues in some form. So the original channel numbers were carried over. Unfortunately for the board operator the work was merely displaced, and the Apollo homework was to copy levels over from the original show to their new lamps and numbers. When the production subsequently went on a national tour it was re-lit from scratch with, this time, a soft-patch.

Replotting

With the rig focused and the patch loaded, the disc went in and the show came back. We plotted and checked levels from the stalls, and all looked fine. Over the week of previews I watched first from the side seats in the stalls, and then the centre seats, and worked my way to the top tier. In the stalls, with moderate attention, the levels from the Tricycle were bright enough, but to move further away, as the majority of the audience were, more light was needed. So for each tier, notes were made to boost some levels because I wanted the audience to see the play clearly. From the back of the third tier they are not so much wondering about the lovely shading of the paint around the doorway, as simply watching the whole, and hopefully being enthralled by the story.

So the new, brighter version of *The Price* opened in September 2003 and ran until mid-January 2004. It was the most successful West End play at the time, and Warren Mitchell was nominated for an Olivier award. And in autumn 2004, starting in Cambridge, the production toured for another twelve weeks.

A Lie of the Mind by Sam Shepard for Dundee Repertory Theatre

This play has been described as an epic, and for good reason, as the setting switches from California to Montana, from comedy to tragedy, and it plays for over three hours. The text unravels families and relationships, and explores 'the American dream'. Shepard gives a very detailed description of how the set was in the original New York production. Of course this description does not have to be followed, and indeed wasn't by the designer, Neil Warmington, who produced an exploded geometric set, which offered a visual puzzle to the audience that almost begged to be pieced back together throughout the play. The geometry created frames, whether flat defined areas on the floor or raised above, as a vertical advertising hoarding.

In the text Shepard has also written many lighting effects into the scene notes – references to moons, changing colours, pools of light, colours of light, practical lights – and these do require following to some extent, because of the physical mechanics of the play. When an actor asked for advice to-wards the rehearsal period, director

continued on page 126

Starker key and side lighting towards the end of the piece, A Lie of the Mind.

Similar high lights used in Duck Hunting. *Lighting by Michael Nabarro.*

OPPOSITE: *Scene from* A Lie of the Mind. *Lighting by Simon Bennison.*

123

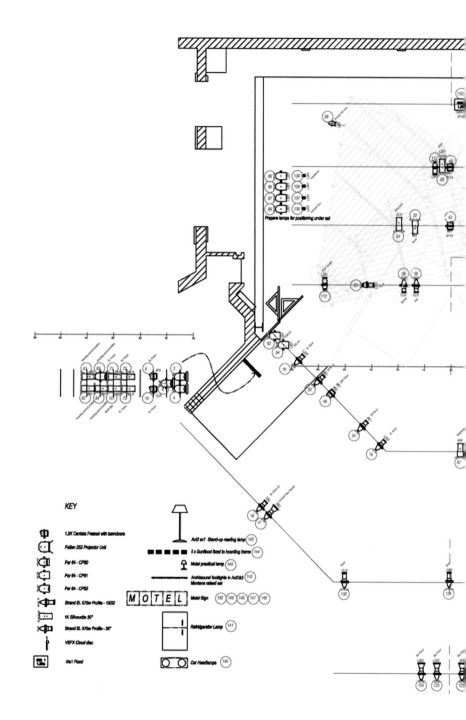

KEY

1.2K Cantata Fresnel with barndoors
Pattern 252 Projector Unit
Par 64 - CP60
Par 64 - CP61
Par 64 - CP62
Strand SL 575w Profile - 15/32
1K Silhouette 30°
Strand SL 575w Profile - 26°
VSFX Cloud disc
Iris1 Flood

Act2 sc1 Stand-up reading lamp (145)

5 x Sunflood fixed to hoarding frame (144)

Motel practical lamp (143)

Architectural footlights in Act2&3 (142)
Montana raised set

MOTEL Motel Sign (150)(149)(148)(147)(146)

Refrigerator Lamp (141)

Car Headlamps (140)

Prepare lamps for positioning under set

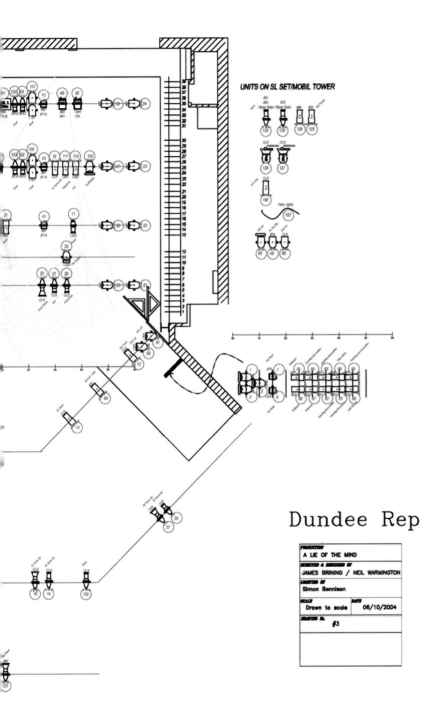

UNITS ON SL SET/MOBIL TOWER

Dundee Rep

PRODUCTION	
A LIE OF THE MIND	
DIRECTED & DESIGNED BY	
JAMES BRINING / NEIL WARMINGTON	
LIGHTED BY	
Simon Bennison	
SCALE	DATE
Drawn to scale	06/10/2004
DRAWING No.	
#3	

125

James Brining commented that, 'It was difficult to tell, until [he] saw the scene with the lights.'

The actor may not have understood that he was indicating the performance in the rehearsal would be shaped by the overall context of how the scene, and the flow of scenes, was sitting on the eye. It was his way of saying, 'I now need to move this to the stage and out of this rehearsal room', and the comment was useful for me because it told me how important the lighting was to be for his overall vision of the production.

The two locations presented the challenge of using different colour-temperature themes to create two different environments. The dominant colour of the set was a dusty desert, turnpike-baked yellow. A deliberate decision on my behalf was to use Rosco gels only: an all-American play needs to be lit with USA colour. There were further reasons for this decision, as the Rosco gels did provide good shades for the colouring of the design; thus #07 was used for a warm colour on the floor and for providing heat for California. The balance for this and for Montana had to be #61. Sometimes you can find it is difficult to mix shades from different colour ranges. A quality and a character come with a gel, which sometimes is just

not right. The Rosco gels offer lighter, seemingly more delicate colours that sat on the set better, and provided the textures needed to light through three hours of scenes.

The design of the set made focusing difficult, with the rake and a raised room that had two positions; the positioning of the lamps reflected this. The front-of-house lighting bridges also became very important locations because they were the most accessible positions during a technical, when sometimes you need to get a lamp in place, and quickly.

What the technical week threw up for me was how the use of scrollers (*see* page 71) must be handled carefully. The low proscenium position was going to be important for lighting across into scenes quite powerfully. The theatre had a set of house scroller strings, which also used all Rosco gel. However, after the plotting session it was discovered that perhaps only one colour out of the string had actually been used, so the scrollers were de-rigged and a single gelled lamp hung instead. It proved that having a choice of instant colours does not make a design – there has to be a reason for specifying a colour scroll, or hiring a moving light. You must clearly decide the effect you are to achieve.

HOME BY DAVID STOREY FOR THE OXFORD STAGE COMPANY

Oxford Stage Company, under the guidance of Dominic Dromgoole, forged a reputation recently for reviving rarely performed, although essential, twentieth-century plays. The work of playwright David Storey has been a focus for this, and especially so after a successful restaging of his play *The Contractor*. In October 2004 *Home* was revived, opening at the York Theatre Royal, which was significant, as Storey hails from Wakefield. The play was originally directed, as with most of his work, by Lindsay Anderson, and had Sir Ralph Richardson and Sir John Geilgud in the major roles.

Hugely successful, the play transferred to the West End and then Broadway, winning plaudits and praise along the way. The original lighting was by the late **Andy Philips**.

The action for *Home* is set largely in real time, in the gardens of a retirement home, although the setting is ambiguous at the beginning of the piece, and it is in fact superbly abstract in requiring only a table and, for the most part, two chairs as the scenery. The text makes references to clouds and shadows, and possibly rain; however, after examination of the characters, because we do not

The appearance of filter G525 on skin.

fully know if what they are saying is true, then we also need not respond by representing clouds or shadows in the set or presentation.

As a result, one can assume that it is only necessary to light the space for its duration, in accordance with it being an outdoor English afternoon. Even Storey himself in rehearsals turned to me and commented, 'Not much to do in this one!' For me, though, this sets alarm bells ringing, with the adage about 'no such thing as an easy job'.

The set design was by Anthony Lamble, and he produced a gently raked, green-grass surface, with two further small rises in level as it progressed upstage. The patination of the grass was subtle, and within the shades of the green there were lighter yellows in the centre and around the table. The whole floor was shaded black around the perimeter. To frame it were three hard, thick-edged portals covered with a dark green serge and having a wonderful perspective and architecture. The final portal itself framed an opera light blue plastic backdrop, with a mist green and blue sharkstooth gauze in front. The only further scenery was upstage right – a section of stone balustrade and paving as the entrance to and from the country house/home, and an old white wrought-iron

round table, with two matching chairs, and then two further rattan chairs placed downstage, right of centre.

The lighting for a set such as this can be made difficult by over-complication. Two factors helped form concepts for design: one was the straight lines of the portals, the other the open space of the stage. It occurred to me that the space could be lit as for dance, not only because it would be the easiest way to fill the void with light, but because the way the stage space is used for dance would suit the architecture and the dynamic of the set.

The colouring used was informed by the need to create a sense of the exterior. I used a mixture of colour corrections, with the idea that throughout a day the light shifts through many colour temperatures (see page 33); also the Rosco blues offer misty shades that reminded me of the plastic backdrop. Therefore I settled on lighting from above in #63, a pipe-end wash in #66, and from the front in #61. The Lee corrections have more red in them, which is good for skin tones, so I also used L202 from the front, and L201 as the backlight. I used the Lee because I also wanted to provide a bridge in colour combinations between the Roscos as the main wash colour, and using L161 exclusively as

127

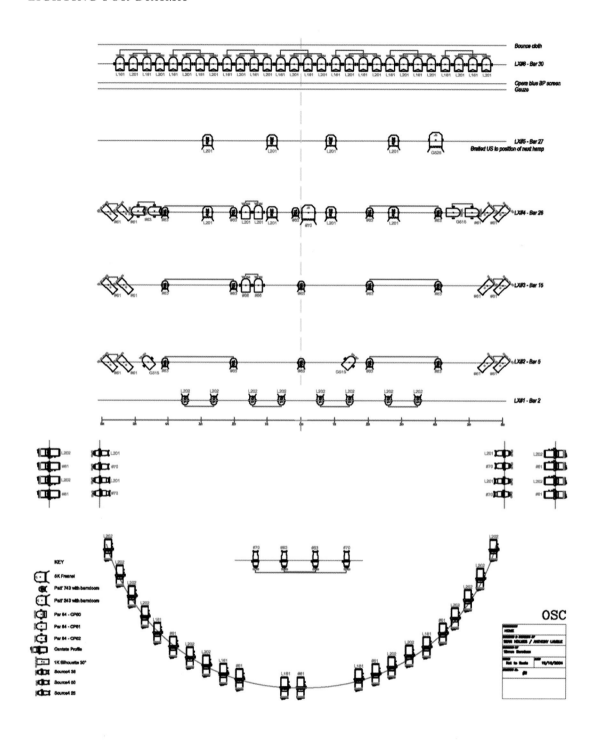

Light plot for the OSC revival of Home *at York Theatre Royal.*

the daylight Par blue of the cyc. The plastic was lit with a bar of Par 64s pointing straight down, with a bounce cloth directly upstage of them. The units had two cuts of L228 in opposing directions, as well as the L161. The effect of this is to provide a really powerful quality of light and an even coverage.

The need to provide a warm wash for balance was avoided by careful placement of lamps through knowledge of actors' blocking from rehearsals, and employing two GAM colours in the specials: G525 was placed in a 5K unit positioned USR on the last pipe, and keyed into centre stage. This lifted the centre of the stage area, heightened the lighter yellows in the floor, and provided a backlight when characters walked between the table and the steps. The G515 was used in parcans, which acted as specials for entrances on the balustrade rostrum USR in the last entrance. There were high side lights on the table, which also lifted to cover characters standing on either side of it; also a pair of parcans acted as a backlight on this area. The GAM colour was chosen even though it has a slight green hue; it comes up warm in a tungsten lamp. This quality works almost subliminally, and

in choosing a warm from the green family it mixed well with the greens in the set and legs. L103 may have worked perfectly well here also, but from my point of view somehow did not belong to the same aesthetic.

The green serge could not be ignored, and was lit with profiles from the front, and focused to the legs in #70 and #63.

The pre-set offered a chance to let the audience walk into the space looking at a different language to the one that they would sit watching the play in. It was therefore lit with the stage completely dark, except for a #66 top light par on the table and a #63 pipe-end parcan on the balustrade.

The legs were lit in #70, and the plastic from the front with two units in L115. The effect was to heighten the green, yet to use shades that melded with the corrections of the main stage state. These colours worked, and the lights largely played at the top end of their levels. The main state dipped 5 per cent in between scenes in Act 1, and then 15 per cent for a check-down towards the end of the play.

The revival was successful, and it is to be hoped that the lighting played its part in this.

Home *required a bright, well-lit feel of the outside.*

12 LIGHTING FOR DANCE

In many ways lighting for dance offers a greater freedom to the designer than does a scripted piece of drama. And with dance you are often dealing with something brand new – innovative choreography perhaps – without the limitations of text, and without scenes and acts. In their place there may be sections instead, but there is essentially a flow of creativity, of movement and ideas. And as a lighting designer this is a gift given to you to interpret.

In lighting a dance piece, the role of the lighting designer can move one or two places up the design ladder. The hierachy can be the choreographer, designer (often a composer), and then the lighting designer. However, there are also many instances where this is scaled down to simply choreographer and lighting designer.

LIGHT FROM DARK

For most presentations dance takes as its starting point the empty 'black box', where everything emerges from darkness, from the blackout. A standard stage set-up would be a 10sqm floor area, laid with a black lino dance floor covering the entire area. On either side of the stage will be four black masking legs, hung above will be black borders, whilst upstage a full black backdrop will create what is commonly called a 'black box' space. With the house lights out, the stage space becomes as dark as possible – and the piece can begin.

Generally with modern dance we are in the realm of the contemporary, so there are no rules to presentation, or in fact for the material itself. In this art form the lighting designer is integral to the

OPPOSITE: **Asyla.**

presentation of the piece, and can afford to think in terms of dressing the stage to the limits of their imagination: enter torches, overhead projectors, digital projection, in fact projection of all types – anything, really, that emits or reflects light.

Imagine our dance space in blackout and the piece about to begin – let us consider a range of alternatives for the beginning of a piece. A pinpoint of light fades up over ten seconds, focused exactly on centre. Alternatively the light could be a large pool, focused hard-edged. It could be a square, a rectangle, a strip of light, horizontal or vertical. The light could fade up slowly or quickly, with or without music, with or without overt shape, with or without obvious colour.

Let us now change the environment, and add to our black box a lino floor in white, or grey. There could be no masking at all; there may be a plastic cyclorama and a gauze upstage in front of it. The gauze could be coloured, or we could put colour on the plastic 'cyc' behind, and this light could be coming from the top or the bottom of these elements, and spread to cover the whole stage.

The opportunities for invention here are many, even within the confines of using just lino, masking and simple cloths. The only rule is that, whatever the elements, they should combine to become both new and original, and, deriving from a new given set of opportunities or themes, be 'right' for the moment.

In dance a lighting designer can hope to realize work that is truly original and creative when, as often happens, a genuine new idea is introduced into the stage space that can inspire and create wonder. For one production at The Place Theatre in London, **Charles Linehan** took the dance space, stripped out all the masking and painted it

Dancers can appear to be almost suspended in light. From Katharsis. *Lighting by Nicholas Phillips.*

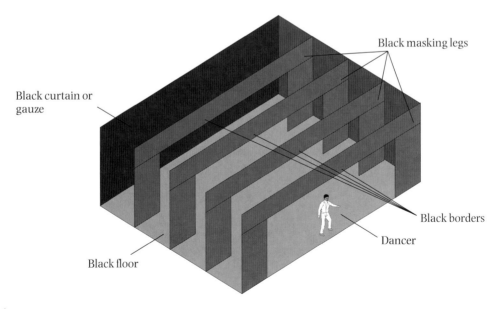

A dance 'black box' space with four 'bays'.

completely white. Had it been done before? I don't know, but the effect, in the change in perception of what you were used to looking at in that space, was inspired.

As with the appeal of works of art in galleries, one of the roles of dance is to communicate to us in an attractive and stimulating manner an understanding of abstract movement, and this in turn informs us at an emotional level about both the world around us, and our inner selves. By turning the kaleidoscope just a small distance, everything changes.

THE REHEARSAL PROCESS

Part of the great pleasure of sitting in on dance rehearsals is that you often get to witness the material as it is created. No two choreographers are alike, and one should never underestimate the capacity of dancers for sheer hard work and repetition – a movement or a series of moves can be rehearsed over and over and over again. Sometimes the repetitious quality of rehearsal can itself be the spark that leads to new directions, and the action of simply getting a thing right can generate its own layers of creativity. A choreographer such as **Kim Brandstrup**, for example, allows for a lot of creativity on behalf of the dancer, which he then moulds and integrates into a work, whereas one such as **Fin Walker** can spend what seems a huge amount of time to a designer on intense small movements, spending hours on what could be only brief moments in the final work.

For the lighting designer you need to see, as with drama, finished runs of dance sections, or the finished piece itself. As good as it is to be in rehearsal, the issue of not seeing a run until the end of a rehearsal period amplifies the problem of having a deadline for handing in a finished drawing to the chief electrician – if your lights are derived from the movement, and you don't know what the movement is going to be, then you can be in trouble! And, as we have discussed before (*see* page 41), the way around this is through good communication.

COMMUNICATION

It is true to say that, over time, the development of a good working relationship with a choreographer goes a long way to solving this problem. Lighting designer **Peter Mumford** works extensively with **Siobhan Davies**, and their working relationship can in many ways be described as symbiotic.

Often the process starts with an early conversation between lighting designer and choreographer, where agreement is reached on what the lighting dialogue of the piece is going to be. This can establish something as simple as making the piece dark and atmospheric. This is not to say that such a question is asked directly, but information such as this can be gleaned early on, and will certainly affect your approach to the final lighting.

For some designers, lighting is part of the rehearsal process. **Michael Hulls** and **Russell Maliphant** will spend time choreographing and sketching in actual lights, when time and money allow, Maliphant working with the light as Hulls designs. Sometimes a complete idea is formed in this way – as in a piece called *Shift*, which evolved from the seven profiles units that happened to be in the studio and were placed on floor stands downstage on the apron. The design was not there at the beginning, yet from two artists daring to say, 'What if we do this?', a clever lighting idea involving brilliant shadow play emerged (for more on *Shift* and Michael Hulls' lighting, *see* page 137).

Cathy Marston is a choreographer who likes to know fairly extensively what the lighting is going to be like at the outset, and this then informs her ideas and thoughts for each new work. Lighting talked about at such an early stage of the process can often have a graphic influence in producing a visual design for the stage floor, or it can fix a location – such as a room. Visual graphics are used in Marston's choreography so much that if you have talked about a light being down left, then it had better be there when you come to light, as she will more than likely have choreographed specifically and precisely for it.

LIGHTING RIGS FOR DANCE

As dancers work from a vocabulary of positions and method, so we can apply a 'basic' or 'standard' lighting dance rig to our 'black box' space, and certainly this basic rig is one from which a lot of dance lighting does originate. It is based on a system of organized 'washes' that enable the creation of multiple options for lighting a dancer in any part of the stage. Such a rig breaks down into the following component parts:

• Top light
• Backlight
• Side light
• Front-of-house

Top light

This provides the main area lighting, and usually divides the stage area into nine points. This divides into three units downstage, three mid-stage, and three upstage. With all of these lamps on separate channels you have control of the centre from down- to upstage, and can light in any combination; for example, if you want a band of top light upstage, then you use just those lights.

Backlight

This can either operate from one bar all the way upstage, or be split into another bar mid-stage. You would do this either on a technical basis, because of the amount of equipment available, or according to the relationship of bars to borders when masking. If we follow the logic already set up, then ideally there is a minimum of three units again to control stage left, centre, and stage right. This therefore becomes another wash or three potential specials.

If we pause here for a moment we can already see that we have nine top light units and say six backlights, providing two washes or fifteen specials. If we then cast an eye back to the list of options at the beginning of our fictional dance piece, you begin to get an idea of the logic of the dance rig and the creative options it is designed to give.

Side light

This is the most important lighting position for dance. Whereas when lighting the actor for drama

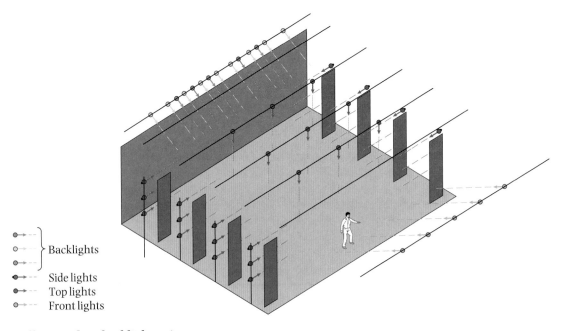

Backlights
Side lights
Top lights
Front lights

Different colour backlight units.

too much shadow can be our enemy, in dance greater amounts of shadow can work for us. The shadows become dramatic, and side light is the best angle for sculpting and moulding the contours of the body. Unlike with drama we are not obsessed with seeing the performer's face; indeed, in all of our angles so far we have not lit the face, but instead have strived to make the whole body clear and attractive, and hence the dance look good.

Overhead we have four bars so far, as the illustration shows (see page 134). Taking an imaginary line down from the end of these pipes to the stage reveals our sidelighting boom positions. If we are using masking, then we create four 'bays' each side for these upright bars – a 'boom' in each bay.

On a dance lighting boom you can find any number of instruments. Jennifer Tipton speaks of lighting and touring whole pieces with just eight instruments, four each side on stands; more commonly you would find a minimum of three units per boom. Lighting dance is about the body, and the boom lamps mirror this, with one unit at low shin height, one at waist/midriff height, and one at shoulder/head height. This is not to say we are only lighting these parts of the body with them. The units still operate as wash lamps, or on separate channels again, as specials. What these units will do, however, is to pull focus in the way that any lighting angle or direction does – for example, the visual feel of all the low shin-height lights in use and lighting a dancer is dramatically very different to the head-high units being in use, although each wash on its own still effectively lights the performer.

After we have constructed a rig out of all these dramatic angles, the last position to include is front-of-house: this is where we need units that will allow us to soften the shadows, light the space and see the faces (yes, if necessary, even if it is just for the curtain call!).

With all the described elements combined, we now have what could be termed as a 'basic dance rig', which takes therefore a 'standard' focus. From this rig some 'looks' have been used so much they too have also possibly become rather 'standard' – for example, using all the lower sidelights as a

wash to make dancers appear to float above the darkness of the black floor space. This effect is re-interpreted in many, many pieces the world over, and a lighting designer with a standard rig now needs to becomes an expert at reinvention, and have a solid knowledge of how to light dance, based partly on what is expected.

Cues

When watching a dance piece it is easy to get carried away with all manner of lighting cues from visual prompts, such as when performers go down right we light them there, and then add another cue for them travelling up left, and so on. Taken this way the notebook will be filled in no time, and the lights would be changing every ten seconds or so. Naturally any dance piece can in essence be very fluid and frantic, so, as with many things, a guiding concept is, once again, 'less is more'.

Just as with a play, so with dance, there are points to be discovered within the visual and musical information, on which you can hang lighting cues. Probably most important in seeing these issues to a satisfactory conclusion is the manner in which you make the notes, based on a thorough knowledge of the structure within any piece. This structure, this skeleton of form, is what you will work with in order to flesh out and reveal the piece in its entirety.

Colour

When applying colour to a dance rig we return to our basic design. What has been described so far in rig terms, as in the diagram on page 134, could be described as a generic nuts-and-bolts reduction of what a contemporary dance rig could be. Dance companies the world over will have variations on a theme of this tailored to their individual needs and repertoire.

What determines the colour used in a play ranges from the time of day, location, country, and the situation as well as the mood. For a contemporary dance piece the designer is freed of most of these restrictions and can concentrate on just one, namely mood. In some instances you can use whatever colour you care to. You could argue also that if you throw enough conviction into any idea, then it will work. The danger is that the lighting can end up becoming just a collection of lights and 'looks', all in place merely for the sake of it. Whatever is placed on the stage, however, it is always better in true design terms when it is rooted in sound thought and decision making. And if you don't agree, then it is time to pass theatre by and head straight for rock and roll, probably collecting a rig of vari-lites along the way!

In conversing with a choreographer, the theme of colour is very likely to occur – as we have previously discussed, colour can be seen as having a direct link to our emotions (see page 29). You may have a conversation where certain colours are talked about to provide a theme to a piece, and there may also be costumes that would lend themselves to a range of colours. A possible constant here is that no matter what shades are used, we are still lighting the body and the skin (quite often more of this on show in dance than in drama), and there is a range of colours that are better suited to this than others. So you may want to use more tints and light shades, or you may use saturated gels, but support them with tints or even open white.

An Approach to Lighting Dance

A choreographer, like all directors, has the ability to visualize a production as a whole; they already know what they want it to be like, and they entrust the design team to make that vision a reality. A choreographer also works in a world of music and rhythm, and therefore a dance is often divided into sections and even beats. So, as a song may be in a form of AB AB C AB, a dance piece for a duet could be BG G B BG B G BG, (where B = Boy, and G = Girl). And in this case, on a visual level, you could then assume that you are going to need seven different looks to light the piece. If you transfer this to our black box space and dance lighting rig, then you could light it as follows:

1. Bright top light state
2. Side light colour #1
3. Side light colour #2
4. Bright backlight
5. Side light colour #2
6. Side light colour #1
7. Bright top light state

This is only an example, but it provides a format that has been used successfully for many pieces. The motivation for choosing different aspects of a rig such as this to light a dance piece can be various and, just as with a dramatic piece of theatre, it is important that we do understand our own logic. And the underlying reasons are infinite: the colour and material of the costumes, the colour of skin and of hair. Is there a backdrop? What colours are in the backdrop? And so on. This can be taken further on a technical level: for example, where will it be performed? How much equipment do we have at our displosal? What kind of stage is it? Will the piece tour? How many crew will be there? And so on.

Then you have to add the creative element, as in: 'How do I want it to look?' and 'Why do I want it to look like this?'. Because here also there has to be a reason, a logic. You can use open white backlight and a #80 side light, but not just because it looks good: that way madness lies!

Our text is the movement of the dancers on stage, the areas they explore and the space they carve. The light has to carve space also, on the stage and in the air. The movement choreographed to music has its structure, and so too must the lighting. However, the lighting can also work with the subtext of the piece, explaining the inner rhythms. Yes, there may be changes as one dancer enters and another exits, but there are also changes within movements, and within ideas.

One of the leading lighting designers, at the very top of his craft, is **Michael Hulls**, who works prolifically and consistently with **Russell Maliphant** and **Jonathan Burrows**. His lighting is often referenced, and with good reason, because he considers all these questions and answers them in the simplest and most concise way possible. This lends a purity to his lighting, which communicates with the utmost sincerity.

With his dance pieces there is often a sound collage or sound-scape, and, with almost always no real set to speak of, Hulls' lighting is then required to provide all the visual information for the piece. It thus reveals the dancers, and provides ebb and flow and punctuation to a piece. Here are two examples:

First, in a piece for Jonathan Burrows, performed on a white dance floor at the Place Theatre in London, the lighting consisted of two top washes of L197 focused perfectly, and inset approximately 1m from the edge of the dance floor. All masking was stripped back, and the dancers wore simple costumes of black and white, almost contemporary Balanchine. The sections were lit in different combinations of the two top washes. Because it was all the same colour, the particular shade became of secondary importance in the lighting to the actual intensity – in effect creating markers in the piece – with lighting states comprising anything from 15 units at 10 per cent to 30 units at full. The lighting, although appearing very simple, still exhibited a richness of quality and a strong ability to communicate the ideas within the piece. It remains a perfect example of minimalist design.

In the previously mentioned *Shift* for Russell Maliphant, a solo created in the late 1990s, Hulls used seven profiles on floor downstage on the apron front. The lamps were focused to large rectangular panels placed side by side on a white cyclorama upstage, and with the addition of a simple side light. However, the lamps downstage were not focused 'straight on', but crossed over the stage in diagonals. So, depending upon where Russell positioned himself – whether up- or downstage, or left to right – the size and number of shadows of his body altered from one to four; so at times the piece became not just a solo but a quartet, danced with copies of himself. It was a brilliant concept, achieved entirely through light, and bringing to the stage a sense of real visual poetry.

Caliban and Sycorax in **Before the Tempest.**

BEFORE THE TEMPEST, AFTER THE STORM AND ASYLA AT THE LINBURY THEATRE, ROYAL OPERA HOUSE, COVENT GARDEN

INTRODUCTION

Choreographer **Cathy Marston** trained at the Royal Ballet School and has danced with Zurich Ballet and Kim Brandstrup, amongst others. In 2003 and 2004 the Royal Opera commissioned new British operas, for which Cathy was asked to choreograph accompanying or 'sister' dance pieces, to be performed at the Linbury Theatre. In 2003 it was *Sophie* based on the novel *Sophie's Choice* by William Styron, and in 2004 pieces based on Shakespeare's *The Tempest*.

Cathy's concept for the latter of these was to provide two pieces, the first of which was also split into two duets, called *Before the Tempest* and *After the Storm*. The first told the story of the birth of Caliban by Sycorax, and how he was cast into the wilderness (or his island). And the second was a piece for Prospero and Ariel, in which the master eventually sets his sprite free into another world. The second piece was called *Asyla*, and was a quintet set to a piece of music by Thomas Ades of the same name. Ades was also the composer of the opera of *The Tempest* that was taking place on the main stage. This provided another link/balance between the two events.

This was the seventh piece for Cathy, so there was a solid working relationship to underpin it, which made for design discussions that were honest explorations of visual ideas and inform-ation, rather than explorations of who we were, and how we worked. For our previous pieces the lighting concepts had led the way. Once the design for the light had been set, it was used to create a structure or an architecture for Cathy to choreograph around. As this then developed, and ideas were hung around each element of the piece, so the connection between light and music became interdependent. For both opera-affiliated projects, the team was completed by designer **Jon Bausor**.

Before the Tempest and *After the Storm* had as a setting a mirrored floor with a canvas and appliqué backcloth, suggesting the underside of the earth or ground as seen from below. This cloth also had a doorway in it, which rolled up via pulleys and revealed what appeared to be a grass surface on the other side, as above the ground, and thus a doorway to another world.

The set design for *Asyla* presented a series of five light wires, a luminescent wire material glowing with electrical current. One wire was designated for each dancer, and all arranged in a 'cat's cradle' and designed to move and stretch within the piece via connections to flown scenery bars. The wires also had vanishing points into the wings where they were fixed via bungee elastic to the wall; thus a dancer could hold a light wire and then pull and interact with it during the piece. This was a complete fusion of dance, design and light.

There was a critical moment in the last design meeting we had for the duets where we discussed whether the backcloth should be hung straight on or at an angle, with the mirrored floor being offset accordingly. Agreeing to this idea made the piece 100 per cent more difficult to design, but spatially it would look better. Cathy and I have this running joke where she asks, 'Can we do it?' and I pause and say emphatically, 'Yes!'

OPPOSITE: Ariel and Prospero in **After the Storm.**

BEFORE THE TEMPEST AND AFTER THE STORM

DESIGNING THE RIG

The Royal Opera House 2 (ROH2) has world-class facilities, but all other elements are budgeted, and this includes the time available. On this occasion, for the first time when working with Cathy, I was in the position of not having designed the lights prior to the rehearsal. It was a most alien feeling because the approach had shifted to that of working with other choreographers. My previous experiences told me that a dance piece is worked on and developed until the very last moment, so I would not get to see a run-through before the lighting plan was due in. This can mean you do not really know the complete work you are about to light even as you draw up the plan, and as such you do not know your text. This can naturally make the act of creating the lighting very challenging.

The method changed accordingly, and the first step was to invest in a video: what is now an indispensable item for all choreographers and dancers, became an essential item for the lighting designer also.

Often when designing a piece there seems to be only one way to do it, and you get it either right or wrong. Perhaps like the sculptor who claims the form was already held within the wood or marble. Applying this idea to lighting means that, whilst you may consider having a row of units in this colour or that, somewhere within all the deliberation there is an ideal and correct way to achieve the required look.

Of course, differing scales of approach also dictate the end result: for a piece for Siobhan Davies, **Peter Mumford** hung five bars of around twenty or so profiles, each focused vertically to create rectangles. It looked fantastic, but was one heck of a focus and rig! For the Cathy Marston evening, because the works were two distinctly different pieces, two rigs had to be put up in the air. Earlier in the season, in a triple bill of Marston revivals, combining rigs had made life very difficult because of the sheer number of instruments. So size of rig was a factor to be controlled.

There is an Auden poem called *The Mirror and the Sea* that is based on *The Tempest* and was also used as research material, with 'the mirror' contributing to the mirrored dance floor. There was also a continuing theme of moonlight, which needed to be expressed for the first duet especially.

Approaching the offset square of lino, what was really required was an offset square set of pipes (bars) overhead to hang profiles on. Because this was not possible, the thought grew to use a single source that could cover the whole area. It was also important for the edges of the dance floor to be defined, and for there to be no spill beyond. This in turn meant having to think about how the lights were going to cover dancers to the very edge of the area.

While carefully focused fresnels could have done this job, what was really needed was the precision of a shutter edge, and the most effective unit really to do this, and give the ethereal glow of moonlight, was a wide-angle HMI profile. This went into the design as a back-/top light to fill the square of mirrored surface, and became the first lamp in the design (*see* illustration).

What is clear for this example is how technical problems and the knock-on effect of choosing units sometimes unavoidably come first, yet effective design is still created. Throughout all this process the videoing of rehearsals still continued, and remained a vital source of information. The taped sections of dance allowed for the creation of a cue synopsis, and snapshots from the tapes to create a storyboard.

So the movement is being watched, understood and absorbed in a parallel stream of thought where the designer can be thinking, 'Okay, to achieve this I'll need to do that, if I want to light this section like so, then I'll need to do this...', and so on. So what a drawn design comes to represent is a toolkit of instruments that will allow for the finished piece to be put together. And even if the overall concept for the finished piece appears far from clear at this

Set model shots of After the Storm *and* Asyla *designed by Jon Bauser.*

stage, the design as rigged and focused will contain all elements to get the job done.

This design needed to provide a general cover over the dance area hung on the imaginary suspended square. As in Dundee with its systems of par lamps (*see* pages 103/104), positions were picked to mimic such a square overhead, and once again profiles were used, this time seven Source 4 50-degree profiles (*see* illustration). The spread of the beam ensured a smooth cover, the shutters a hard cut, and their position that the dancers would be lit to the edge of the stage, with the beam still crossing above head height at centre.

For the opening sequence of the first duet, total darkness was required to emphasize the impact of the opening of the sound score – a manipulated series of screams, analogous to the birth of Caliban. Sycorax is discovered sitting on the shoulders of Caliban, who in turn is hidden by her costume. The effect was pure theatre, with careful low-level sidelighting disguising the full form of the two bodies. It was important to maintain the low level of light for the opening until after the 'birth' of Caliban, who emerged from under her gown. This point was anticipated in the cueing when the HMI profile opened up for the first time.

This side light was the first series of lanterns put into the design for the boom positions (*see* illustration). Other units for the plan followed suit after this: more side light would be required throughout for colour shifts within the piece, and a front wash focused into the square of the dance surface.

Out of rehearsal there were other moments that Cathy said she would need 'to see' – to light specifically. This kind of clarity is useful, because you can then act straightaway on it and include it in the design. One such request was to catch Caliban and Sycorax as they looked into the distance – 'To the shore? To the island?' – upstage left. This became another job for the booms.

A feature of the set design was a roll of turf, positioned two-thirds of the way downstage on the stage right quarter and in line with the hidden doorway. Both duets began at the turf, the first also ending at it. A Strand beam light and a 1.2K PC were added to the design, both of which could be tight-focused to the same spot (*see* illustration). The PC was to act as a 'halo' around the narrower beam light; this was once again to be a reference to moonlight.

continued on page 144

OVERLEAF: *Early overhead light plot layout for* The Tempest/Asyla *bill.* Asyla *lanterns in blue.*

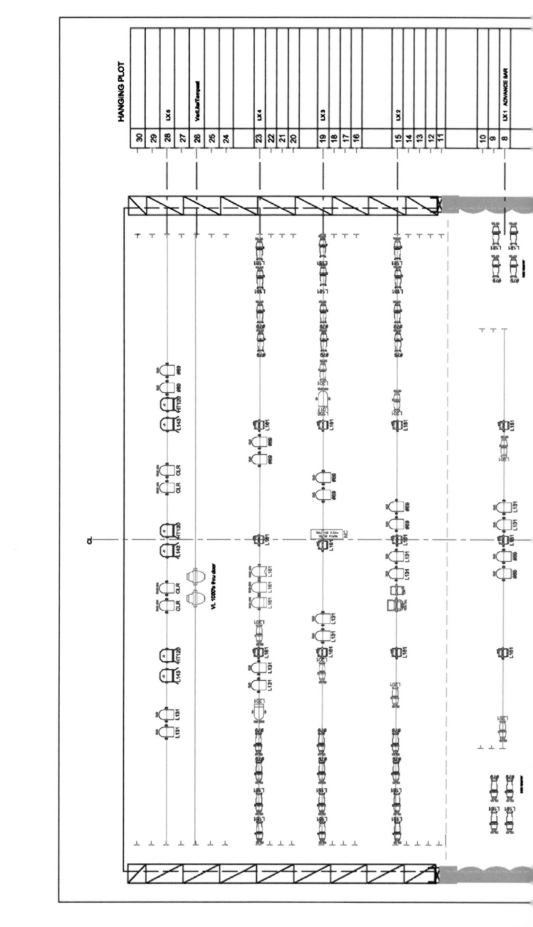

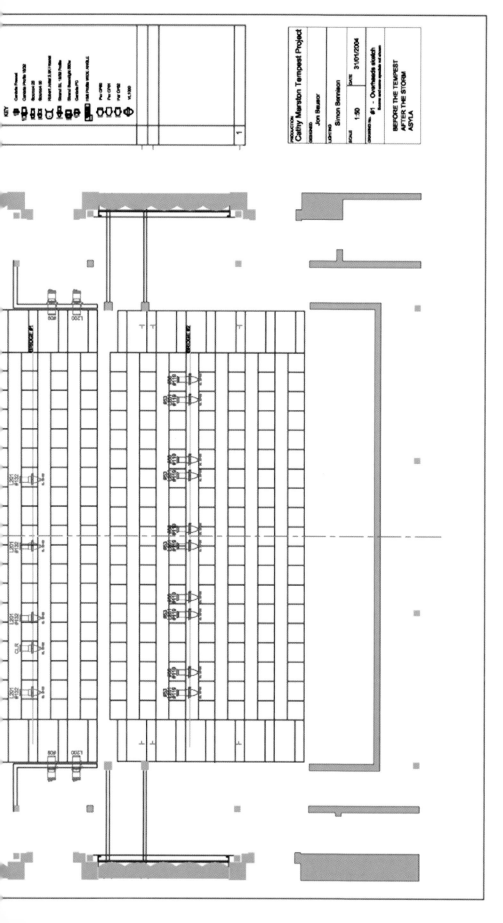

KEY

PRODUCTION:
Cathy Marston Tempest Project

DESIGNED:
Jon Bausor

LIGHTING:
Simon Bennison

SCALE: 1:50   DATE: 31/01/2004

DRAWING No: #1 - Overheads sketch
Scene and some symbols not at scale

BEFORE THE TEMPEST
AFTER THE STORM
ASYLA

Within the choreography taking shape in rehearsal there became apparent a strong use of one particular diagonal running from upstage left towards the turf roll. If, when watching a dance piece, a diagonal lighting system were added to the lighting plan every time the dancers moved in that direction, there would certainly not be enough lamps on the kit list to do this, nor enough time to focus them. However, on this occasion it seemed such a strong element that it was included, together with the notion that the units could also be used for specials should they not be needed for the diagonal. Four medium parcans were thus drawn in a position upstage, and continuing mid-stage (*see* illustration on pages 142–43).

For the second duet, there was a moment when the doorway needed to appear slowly and the turf rolled out towards this other world of bright daylight. Upstage of the door was a small back plastic. The designer determined that if the backcloth represented the underside of the earth, it followed that the plastic should be the sky: thus another design decision was made for the plastic to be lit a sky blue.

A late request was for there to be a column of light – bright sunlight – moving like a sundial around from stage left to the line of the turf pathway. With the set having been twisted through 30 degrees or so from the natural square of the stage space, not only was masking more of an issue, but also, for this particular effect, the opening through the doorway had become narrower. A moving light (*see* page 71) with shutters seemed to be the obvious key to solving this problem, as it would allow for the creation of the column of light and its subsequent need to pan across the stage. What a luxury to be able to think like this with our new lighting technology! After looking at sections and angles it became apparent that with the door opening narrower, one lamp panning was not going to be enough – indeed, the whole effect was risky. However, having secured a second moving light for the rig, it seemed that some semblance of the desired effect would be possible.

Colour and Set Dressing

With a play there is often a need to describe the passage of time using light; with this piece there was a similar need to indicate a transition from a world beneath the earth to one above. The light in the rig that provided the intensity and colour temperature for other colours to hang around was the HMI profile. In the European opera houses they take this cool quality of light and then offset the Lee corrections against it, often with open white serving as a 'warm' colour. When events turn to the sinister, Lee 117 (steel blue) or 106 (primary red) can come into play. Direct and powerful colour communicates well.

Not being sure how to use the general cover of Source 4 50-degree units set against the HMI, we decided to opt for no colour, the loose theory being that the open white would compliment the cool, and frankly if it did not work, colour could be added! It is important to remember that sometimes lighting is not an exact science – it is too full of creative interpretation and impulse to be thus.

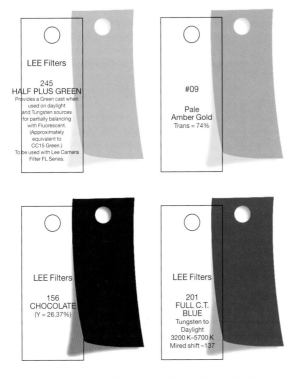

Swatch books – showing colours described in the text.

Fabric samples and a costume drawing. (L.J. Bauser sample for Tempest *and R. Vicky Le Sache sketch for* Mowgli's Jungle.

The front-of-house rig remained open white, and the daylight plastic became a very literal #68 – sky blue. For the opening scene, and the side light for Caliban's birth, L156 (chocolate) was used because of the nature of Lee colour and the effective skin tones it achieves at low levels.

The side light colours, ranging from warm to cool, were to be L245 (half plus green), a light green that appears very warm at a low level before becoming its true shade at full level; L154 (pale rose), to be available for a cleaner skin tone. Finally, L201 (full CT blue), put into the shins and the off-the-floor units to retain cool looks and work with the HMI.

The backcloth also needed to be dealt with. It was a wonderful piece of painting, a deep coppery hue with chunks of earth seemingly clinging to the surface, and it would clearly take dark brown and shiny grey light well. Some units were positioned overhead to glance across and catch details of the appliqué, and then some units were added front-of-house to allow for the changes of colour on the wall if required by the changing action on stage – for this, washes of L106 and 200 (double CT blue) went in, the effect wanted from the cloth being similar to the appearance of the Seagram Rothko's in the Tate Gallery room.

ASYLA

INITIAL DESIGN THOUGHTS

Jon Bausor's exciting design of the five light-wires for *Asyla* created an instantly mouth-watering opportunity to shine all manner of units between the wires to create all manner of patterns and intricacies. And these tantalizing possibilities would be further realized when the wires were moved by the performers during the piece, thereby offering further shapes and angles.

However, as choreographer and lighting designer sat and watched these ideas develop in rehearsal, it became clear that this level of sophistication was simply too complicated. Other factors in play, such as the aural information of the score, the visuals of the light wires themselves, and most importantly the choreography, had to be allowed to speak first; another layer of wonderfully focused and clever light would simply have been too much information. Also of consideration was the time factor for focusing, and as mentioned before, at the time of delivering the plan the piece was still being worked on.

Mark Henderson was responsible for lighting a new production of *The Flying Dutchman* for the Royal Opera, and, being the very busy gentleman that he is, delivered the plan at the last moment. With nothing too specific indicated for the overhead rig at the beginning of the technical Sunday, he turned and said, 'Just focus the rig up to

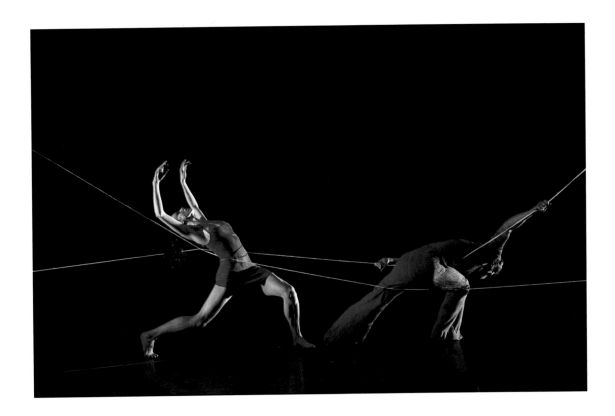

Duet in Asyla *with 'light-wires'.*

your standard settings, then we'll take it from there and see what works.' The sheer logic of what he said made sense, and sure enough, for the lighting of the show, out of a standard repertoire ballet focus, came washes that worked, with some lamps working as specials. And this became a basis for the design that allowed him to light the production very successfully.

After much thought it became clear that the way forward was to light the dance piece and ignore the light-wires – to make a dance rig work and light the stage. This decision provided a release that allowed the nuances in movement to be seen without the clutter of having to think about a complicated set.

The final rig developed into one of a nine-point top wash, with cover front-of-house, a three-point backlight in two colours, and standard side light. The vanishing point of the light-wires to the edges of the stage meant that many moments of the piece came from the centre of the stage; thus an extra par backlight to wash into either side of centre was added.

Specials

Unlike in *Scenes from an Execution* (page 87), the washes from the ballet rig could not be relied on to act as specials for more defined moments. For example, there was a point in the piece where one of the dancers stood and waited on centre before spinning into his next sequence, hinting at an opportunity to add a special above him. In another moment the importance of downstage left was demonstrated. Watching the piece in rehearsal, a pattern emerged that would require support within the lighting. These appear on the plan as CP61 parcans, with beams focused across, and used to lift these moments either on their own or within states – see illustration.

Colour

Jon Bausor, the designer, produced a swatch sheet of the fabrics to be used for the costumes, which is always useful when choosing gel colours. The colour of the light-wires was a vibrant aqua blue, and the network of parcans were gelled in #69 to amplify this. The top light used was L161 (slate

blue), with backlights in L143 (pale navy blue) and HT120 (deep blue) in 2K fresnels. (HT = high temperature – a range of colour designed to cope particularly well with the hotter light sources used in stage lighting.) The extra par backlight remained in OW. The L161 also went front of house, and the boom colours used were #78, #72, L161 and OW. Some of these colours were influenced by the fabric swatch, plus a knowledge of colours that work well together.

Changes from the Original Designs

The final design for the two pieces came together as described above, with many decisions being left until the last moments of drawing up the plan. Certainly, without recording video sections of dance in rehearsal, all decisions for the design would have been far harder.

Thus, although all the ideas that went into the plan had a technical aspect to them or were based on set or costumes, or on themes and ideas – it was also true that they were always decisions based on the piece in front of me, as seen in rehearsal. As it was, the technical week began with a very clear idea of exactly how the rig was to be focused, and what the role of each unit was to be. During the course of the week, naturally, there were changes. Here is some of what happened:

- In the duets *Before the Tempest* and *After the Storm* all the ideas were working well until the first bright state for the birth of Caliban. The Source 4 wash in OW was a good cover for lighting dancers to the edge of the space, but in colour clearly spoke of its 575W tungsten light source. The HMI, on the other hand, had a wonderful colour and quality, but as a single source did not create a cover. In other words, the two did not quite match up. Cathy's comment was, 'Can we make the cover cooler to match the other light?' So the Source 4s became L201, which allowed the HMI to work with them as one wash until the single backlight was needed. It followed therefore that the front-of-house wash became L201 also.

- The units to glance across the appliqué on the backcloth did not work because in practice they made the cloth look like a wrinkly old rag! – they brought out too much texture. So these units were transferred to a front-of-house position, as straight on as possible, so rather than giving texture, the gels revealed the different hues within the cloth. Fortunately it was what Cathy and Jon really wanted to see when they talked about the texture of the cloth, and was probably an area of the design that in hindsight could have been foreseen.

- As already discussed, the Vari-Lite 1000 moving lights were likely to be the Achilles heel of the design and, as such, a worry. The angle of the set proved more problematic than even the sections and angles had shown. After much patience and careful tweaking of blades and tilts, the cue sequence was installed and running. We played it back, we played it back again. By this time the novelty factor had worn off, and still, even after all the effort put in, it simply was not working. Sometimes you just have to let a thing go. The units were still used, though, the first as a shaft of bright daylight at an angle through the door, the second as a backlight cut to the grass pathway. The first then changed position to act as a special top light lighting Prospero standing beyond the door at the end of the piece. Also, the grass pathway did not 'zing' out against the HMI profile, so extra backlight profiles were needed in to supplement the vari-lite.

- In the side light the L156 came out warm enough that the L154 was not needed – a lesson on colour temperature at low level. A colour was needed, however, to lift the look out of the red of the L156 and the cool L201, and for this #09 was added instead. Although only used in a couple of cues, it nevertheless provided what was needed. The #09 was also transferred for a backcloth wash, which again neutralized the look just enough to take the colour balance either way from warm to the cool of the HMI look.

- Jon Bausor the designer had wanted to feature UV in both pieces owing to the nature of some of his costume fabrics; for Aerial's costume there were some screen-printed images of Jenny Tattersall printed directly on to the cloth, as if Aerial's spirit was caught within. The UV, although it worked as a quality of light, did not really sit in harmony with the look of the show. However, it was found to reveal an astonishing patination to the backcloth when used on its own. This effect was thus used for the final image of the second duet, with Aerial caught in a carefully hard-cut side light against the cloth or earth. The UV was turned on in a cue to warm up in time, and snapped out with the next cue as the profile took a fast fade.

- *Asyla* was very successful and everything worked with no gel changes, with all intended lanterns used in the final design. Some side light was added from 1m Thomas M16 battens sat on the floor. These lit underneath the light-wires and in L174 (dark steel blue) stayed just cool enough at low level.

- The light-wires themselves we thought to be dimmable through DMX conversion. When they arrived it was disappointing to discover this was not the case, despite the valiant efforts of the Opera House lighting systems department. This meant that as a creative team we could not 'play' with them as we had hoped, and in the process this probably saved a good few minutes of technical time. Therefore the cues to use these wires all became snaps (0 sec) and we just needed to decide where the snap cues should go and the evolution of their use through the sequence. The snap cues in the end provided another rhythm and dynamic to the already jagged nature of the music score, and actually proved a real boon.

All in all, the pieces with alterations made during the technical and dress rehearsals worked very much to the great satisfaction of the team. The performance is archived after being filmed and broadcast by BBC3.

FEARFUL SYMMETRIES

An aspect of **Peter Mumford's** lighting for dance is how dynamic he is at pulling colour and light around the stage. He won an Olivier award for *Fearful Symmetries* by **Ashley Page** for the Royal Ballet. The music was a score of great momentum by the American composer John Adams, and the pace of the score was transformed into great sweeps in the choreography – and the lighting needed to follow suit.

The set design by **Anthony MacDonald** consisted of only a few elements that provided constant visual change throughout the piece: in a standard black box set-up there was an ink-blue gauze panel downstage, and a flown off-set solid orange square beam mid-stage. Off to stage right, hanging at an angle so the downstage corner was just above head height, was a curved box metal wall faced with painted black ply, with a regular pattern of small holes punched through it. This wall also had a thin yellow flap/line opening out at the upstage corner. Upstage was a deep plum-coloured gauze with an abstract shaded perimeter/rectangle, again not too far removed from Rothko. And for a piece of visual trickery, a fluorescent green rectangular flown panel sat in front of the gauze and began a journey high stage right. By virtue of an ingenious travelling gyroscope-style gadget, the panel slowly rotated along the course of its route to stage left over the duration of the piece.

It was a high quality piece of set design that presented Peter with a huge amount of visual imagery for colour and then ideas. The curved wall on stage left was backlit from the gallery with a 2.5K HMI fresnel; this in turn projected pin-points of light across the floor. The points of light, looking like stars on the floor and in the air, were backed up with a shifting set of colours front-lighting the wall: a deep purple, a yellow and a red, and the colours on the wall combined and shifted as a hanging nebula.

All other scenic elements required adventurous use of colour, and the cues ran, the music chugged, and the dancers swirled through entrances and exits alone or in packs. When using all the saturated gels, there was also a barrage of open white from M16 battens and profiles, sat low on the floor running up- and downstage. So whatever colours were changing in the air and on the set, the dancers themselves could always be clearly seen. And when he needed more colour, followspots were plotted to follow in deep purples and reds.

Summary

The success of Mumford's lighting for *Fearful Symmetries* was the dialogue between the lights and the direction of the dance working together. The colour created another universe for the scenery to exist in; and open white – used to directly light the dancers, aided by dynamic cueing – always focused the eye and kept visual interest throughout. The lighting units and positions were 'standard', but the vocabulary was not; hence he managed to create original work by reinterpreting dance lighting language, and by seeking adventure.

As a lighting designer in dance you have the opportunity to make the lighting move and perform such that it takes a more integral role in the entire creative process. And to achieve this, if it is in the spirit of the choreographer's vision and what is trying to be constructed, there is no set formula: the more you are 'locked-in' with your subject matter, the more you understand it from all points of view, the better the lights shall communicate, and the better a piece shall look.

13 LIGHTING FOR BALLET

Lighting classical ballet is a very different discipline to lighting modern or contemporary dance. And whereas in the previous section dance was described as originating in darkness, so ballet comes from, and is about, light. It is a land of princesses and princes, a world where gravity is cheated, and sparkle, glamour and magic abound. In addition, a ballet dancer has often trained for many hard years to arrive at a standard of technique good enough to get them into a ballet company, and their technique is paramount and needs to be seen, as do in particular their feet and hands.

A ballet company is usually associated with a large opera house and will perform in a large stage space. This space has a lot of air surrounding the dancers, all of which needs lighting; generally speaking, therefore, lighting ballet requires a great many instruments.

THE BALLET RIG

A figure, perfectly well lit in broad sunny daylight, when transposed to the stage requires the same amount of illumination (if not more) to be similarly 'perfectly well lit'. This is, of course, largely impossible in a literal sense, as diffused daylight arrives from every direction. However, we can simulate the multiplicity of those directions by multiplying our lighting angles, positions and options.

If we take the sketch of a standard dance rig compiled for contemporary dance (*see* page 134), it would follow that in saying we need more light

OPPOSITE: **Cinderella Act 3, by Serge Prokofiev for the Royal Ballet, Covent Garden, London.**

we would multiply the number of lights drawn in each position. Therefore a nine-point top light can be supplemented with further top light washes; a pipe-end unit could become a pair of units, and then multiplied by three; and the backlight wash can similarly grow into two or three washes.

In increasing the number of units, and therefore washes, we naturally also increase our colour options. A plan containing three sets of pipe-end units at the end of each bar allows us the use of three different colours and is the norm for the majority of ballet rigs. And if we are using profiles, then one set of these can be used to carry a gobo wash.

Whereas the average modern dance touring boom is moderate in height, a ballet boom is always taller because of the number of units required to provide the colour-mixing options; also because a steeper angle from the boom is required, as it is considered necessary to light the classical dancer in a different manner. Side angles at waist and head height are good, as we have seen, to light a dancer in a sculptural and dramatic fashion. But for a ballerina, the light must not be directly focused at eye height; too many bright lights from this angle can be disorientating and blinding, and can create balance problems, especially during the big numbers. In addition, the dramatic angle in ballet needs to be saved for the dramatic moment, and thus to light the ballerina effectively an angle further up the boom is used, that still sculpts but is kinder to the body and the eye.

If we have multiplied the fixtures in all our washes, of course, this is effective, and still creates very direct lighting. To broaden this out, a ballet rig would also use the natural gaps in the rig drawing – that is, the physical spaces in the theatre between

151

lighting positions; these other positions would be described as follows:

- The **Bridge** or **#1 Spot bar**
- The perch or **Tormentor**
- The **Gallery**
- The **Slips** or **Box boom**
- **Border lights**

For the conceptual dance rig on page 134 in the front-of-house position, we put in some units 'just for the calls'. Now we need to see our dancers clearly, and accordingly the number of lights in this position increases, and with them the available colour options. The front-of-house now becomes an important position. What must be remembered throughout all of this description is, compared

An opera house 'tormentor'.

to modern dance, our theatres are usually much bigger, so the overhead rig has grown by a couple of bars, and our front-of-house 'throw' (distance from unit to stage) is also much greater.

Just as in a play, we cannot push in more light from the front without continuing it on to the stage. Although the theory does not work exactly as a general cover (*see* page 53), this is nevertheless where the 'bridge' or #1 spot bar comes into its own. It is the position where further front washes sit as far downstage as possible to get under the first border of the set, and continue the front wash upstage. The important point of this position is that it also exists in its own right for valuable washes and specials. The bridge can see all manner of gobo washes or special effects rigged from it, and it can also provide anything up to five or six different colour washes. In the US, where the ellipsoidal spot is predominant – that is, less use of fresnel or any other unit – the bar becomes stacked with profiles and is a veritable beast to tour and focus. In many respects the bridge provides a kinder angle dramatically than the real front-of-house, so it is often the first option for a designer when 'adding in fronts'. And, as the dancer moves downstage beyond the bridge position, then the true front-of-house units come into play.

If we now imagine a line taken vertically down from the very ends of the #1 spot bar, we discover a position that exists structurally in most opera houses and is known as the 'tormentor' (so called because it is very close to, and almost touches – or torments – the curtain line and thus the curtain itself). And because this supplies a very useful lighting angle, it is a position that has often been developed into having two or three levels, allowing for multiple instruments to be rigged (*see* illustration).

In an opera house the distance between the first downstage boom and the first front-of-house lamp can be huge. The 'torm', falling between the two, fulfils a lighting role by offering what could be described as a high/side/front lighting position in that it marries together the stage, the FOH and the bridge. The 'torm' can also come into its own as a lighting position, as being the best dramatic angle to light 'into' a set – that is, for a downstage

The gallery, or fly rail.

The 'slips'.

box set, such as the kitchen for the first scene of *Cinderella*, or the forest clearing for the first act of *Giselle*.

This angle becomes even more important when viewed in relation to the position of the instruments front-of-house – because an opera house often has a 'horseshoe'-shaped auditorium, you rarely get a true front-on spot-bar position (this is especially the case in mainland Europe). The front-of-house light actually often comes from a side position around one of the higher tiers of the horseshoe; therefore, if we are using front-of-house washes and want them to go further on to the stage and under the proscenium, then the tormentor becomes the perfect position.

With all these additional lighting positions, what we also now have is a greater range of lighting possibilities, which is exactly what is needed to get through a three- or four-act ballet. But there is more yet...

Looking straight on at the sidelighting boom as through a front elevation, with the overhead electric above it, there is another huge gap where light can be missed. Ideally you would have a complete goalpost of instruments in three or more colours, but what we find instead is the gallery or fly rail. The instruments here can often fall into a bay system, as there is a lighting bar between each border, with a boom underneath; and for each bay there can be instruments above in the gallery. In an established repertoire theatre there can be many lamps, enough for several washes. On tour, however, due to the labour-intensive method of simply getting the lights up there, they may be reduced to a single fixture in each bay. In this situation the gallery may provide an alternative colour wash, or may plug a hole in the cover between the boom and the pipe-end on the overhead pipe. And depending on the wishes of the designer, it could also be the place for a gobo wash.

The 'slips' are a similar 'plugging' position, and can have several names: high sides, box-booms, high slips (*see* illustration). However named, it is usually a position high up, in front of the proscenium, or in an auditorium side box (not such a popular viewing point as it once was, and commonly now turned over to lighting rather than to box-office profit). A true 'high slip' can be a very useful position in its own right, being a long throw at a steep angle, and well able to fill into the downstage for both scenes and specials.

A box-boom, being further round into the auditorium, exists architecturally as a more genuine straight-on position for the front-of-house, and as such can act to link units on the downstage
continued on page 156

OVERLEAF: *Lighting rig for the American Ballet Theater at the Metropolitan Opera House.*

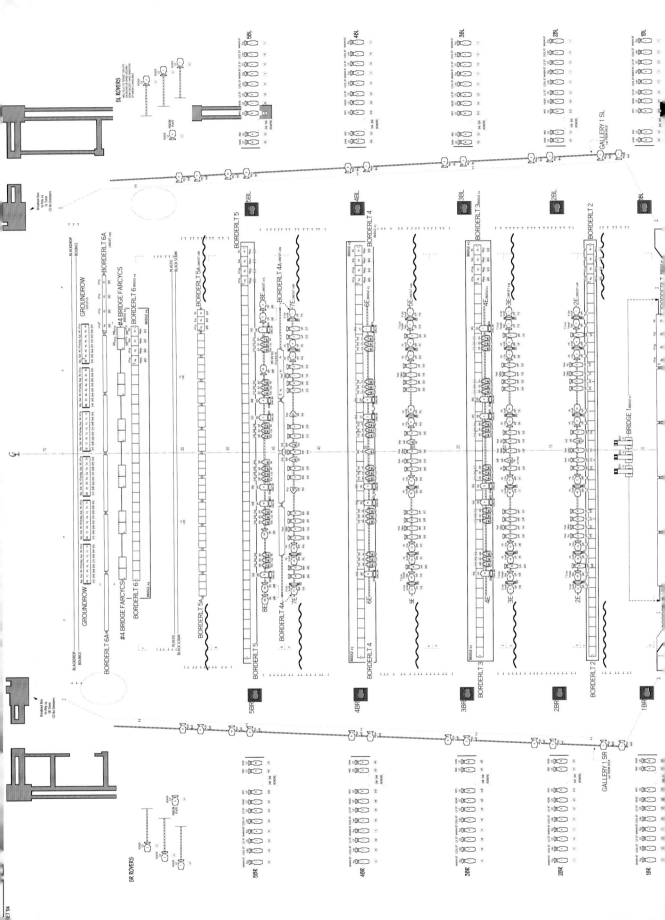

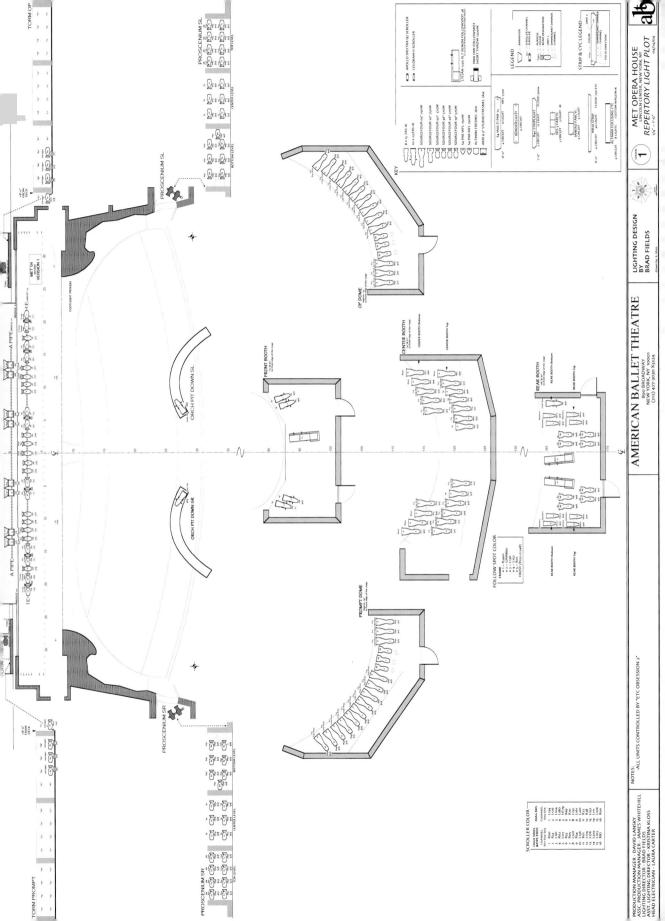

Traditional 'border lights'.

boom, and the tormentor, with the front position. In doing so it adds to the 'cover' units, as well as providing washes or specials of its own.

In the instance of lighting a 'traditional' ballet set, the borders, rather than being black, often become part of the scenery and need to be lit. In this case border lights are added to the overhead rig; in the US they are called 'X-rays'. The bar is usually a pipe as near as possible to, and upstage of, the overhead lighting bar. The units are trimmed just above those on the lighting bar, to allow the light to see upstage and on to the border being lit. The colours used here are very often primary red, blue, green and white, which accordingly can be mixed to light all colours in the scenery (*see* colour mixing on page 30). Sometimes, especially in countries such as Russia and Japan, a bolder approach is used, the white channel being used to take another colour, maybe lavender or yellow. In some cases, and in the larger opera houses where these flood battens are such a permanent fixture, coloured glass has been installed instead of gel, which, considering the turnover of even high temperature saturated gels, seems a very sensible idea.

The lighting rig at this stage is still not complete, because for any design there is usually a need for specific instruments, namely specials. What is evident, however, from this comprehensive rig is that, if not actually all 360 degrees, a great number of lighting angles are available, the aim being to light our dancer well and to bring to vivid life the action on the stage, and, as part of this, the scenery itself.

DESIGNING FOR BALLET

The process of lighting a play, a dance piece or a ballet is the same in terms of thought and approach. All the criteria already described elsewhere, in terms of theory, research, communication and rehearsals, can be followed in the same way – that is, how you arrive at choosing your colours and angles, and how you decide on how the piece is going to look.

Northern Ballet Theatre has for a few years now produced a series of full-length ballets based on famous stories: *Dracula, Frankenstein, Carmen, Wuthering Heights*. This trend provides everyone, most importantly the audience, with a text to follow, and makes research easier. Likewise a familiar score, such as *Swan Lake, Giselle, Sleeping Beauty*, is easier to access than an unfamiliar one. A new composition can make the task a little harder, in that knowledge of the text is compromised by lack of knowledge of the form and tempo of the score. The choreographer, having requested music to last for X number of bars, will have the best idea of how the piece is intended to be – although as a lighting designer you should be on familiar territory and able to cope. You will also have a copy of the music and access to the ideas of the composer, as well as the rest of the production team.

In the case of lighting one of the classics you are potentially overwhelmed with research material, through videos, DVDs, books, and also live performance. What you also find in this case is that the music is in charge, because the score of *Swan Lake* or *The Nutcracker* is the ultimate text, and all the moods and colours, and even the fades, are contained in the music. What you will also find is that there is an orchestra to compete with, and during rehearsal it becomes an unstoppable force of forty plus people who will not pause to see if a cue is better at five or eight seconds.

Another familiar situation when lighting traditional ballets is that they mostly all have a transformation scene or scenes. As a lighting designer it is your job to ensure that they look magical, and to make this harder still you often also really only ever have one chance of getting it right, because of the time restriction. So you have to know exactly what you are trying to achieve, and you have to know your rig – your lighting palette – and how you are going to make your colours and angles work on the scenery and cloths.

The Process of Design

Such is the fast pace of work in the ballet arena that it is important that in designing the rig for a ballet, all stages of design are followed carefully (meaning no errors). It is especially important that the rig is numbered in a fashion that allows for fast and efficient working. When you are working under pressure and want to see all the #80 pipe-ends in blue, call '1 through 20' and they are there, then add in the L161 top light '121 through 135' and these are added. Numbering groups consecutively can therefore really help speed things up, and will prevent you from always having to look at your plan – and most modern lighting systems will allow you to number the circuits however you wish through a 'soft-patch' system, and this will therefore form part of your vital preparation. This system can be followed throughout the rig, and creating such 'groups' is where you also really begin to get a full knowledge of how the rig is working, and how you are going to pull the light around on the stage.

In the USA they approach this in a very technical way and it locks into their popular 'Light Write' program and their general ethos of list making and numbering of lighting rigs. Their system, whereby each unit has its own individual identification number – separate from its channel – may seem complicated at first, but after a period of use it becomes virtually like a stock-taking sheet for a lighting rig, where you can spot and cross-reference information. And when you have a ballet rig of some 500-plus instruments hanging in the air, it can save a lot of head scratching.

In fact, whatever theatre you are in, when lighting for ballet there will nearly always be a highly evolved system of numbering for the rig. The numbers will either run in consecutive lots, or in groups. There will, of course, be quirks in any system: for example, side light numbers hopping across stage, rather than downstage to upstage. Similarly a boom may number 1 through 6 top to bottom, or 301/311/321/331/341/351;

The American method – paperwork.

each company to their own. And should you get paperwork from Germany, it is worth noting that their stage left is our stage right!

Followspots

Finally, the use of followspots must not be underestimated as a dramatic lighting tool for the ballet. Whenever you are in any doubt of being able to see your dancer you can call upon its services, and it is the same whether you need the diamonds to sparkle more or to light with real sensitivity.

One of the unique elements to the lighting of the Royal Ballet's *Romeo & Juliet* is how Juliet is always caught in the followspot. For the operator of the show you virtually dance the steps with her, as you are involved in almost every scene. The followspot is on sometimes when the rest of the stage is in blackout. It is also one of the devices **Kenneth Macmillan** used to carry Juliet through scene changes: for instance, before the last bedroom scene, the lights fade leaving Juliet caught in the spot; she is followed in three increasing circles around the stage, and then runs to the window upstage left as the dawn light comes up through it, and the lights build into the scene.

For the audience this is most thrilling, and causes the same adrenalin rush as do the large transformations – only here they are concentrated down to dancer and followspot. You also have a situation where, rather than working from darkness, the stage has been taken down to darkness – that is, the followspot can allow you to experiment with far more shade and atmosphere in the lighting and scenery, so it becomes a tool for a designer to judge and balance how to light scenes. It can also be thought about as a crucial part of cue planning – that is, you can build how a scene and dancer is lit around the spots, and let your rig light the scenery, knowing full well that the dancers are catered for.

CINDERELLA BY SERGE PROKOFIEV FOR THE ROYAL BALLET, COVENT GARDEN

The lighting of Act 1 of Prokofiev's *Cinderella* has to be one of the most awesome of tasks. The ballet begins, lights go up, and you are in a kitchen: Cinderella with her broom by the hearth. The story develops, and there is the first real lighting moment for the entrance of the Old Crone.

It is all in Prokofiev's score if you listen carefully; the themes for different characters and the various plot moments intertwine and resurface throughout the piece. We hear the theme for the Old Crone's appearance, and you know the lighting has to change, it tells you the look should be mysterious. The action pulls back to the kitchen and, after various entrances, the Crone returns to become the Fairy Godmother. This cues the first transformation, as she takes Cinderella through the seasons, ending in winter. The seasons then return, and at some point towards the end of the scene, a carriage needs to be discovered, and the palace that Cinderella is about to be whisked off to, distantly appears.

This all happens in about thirty minutes, and presents a serious amount of lighting and rapid cueing. As the last person in the artistic process at the point of creation in the theatre, you have to know exactly what is happening as regards the music and the way the scenes are to unfold; together with the orchestra, the lighting is driving the ballet along.

Certainly it is important to get the cues you need into the lighting board as quickly as possible at the outset, as then it will be all the easier to watch and make notes. And notes are vital and often your only weapon, because, unlike a drama where the

From **Cinderella** *by Serge Prokofiev for the Royal Ballet, Covent Garden.*

'tech' can be stopped for you – *see* page 82, in ballet the music and the changes are unstoppable, there is simply not time to dwell, and the lights need to be in the board plotted, and you able to move on.

This act of *Cinderella* is possibly about as fast-paced as it gets, but all ballets have their big scenic moments: the entrance of Carabosse in the Prologue of *Sleeping Beauty*, Rothbart and the Black Swan in Act 3 of *Swan Lake*, even the storm sequence in *La Fille Mal Gardée* – otherwise quite a gentle piece. And you will find they happen either quickly or at the end of an act, so during rehearsals, when typically with ballet lighting you are required to plot your cues, you get only one chance of seeing the sequence in action.

Summary

As we have seen, the process of lighting for classical ballet is one step removed from that of modern dance, and perhaps two from that of straight drama. Nevertheless, our thought patterns, and the theories that lie behind many of our decisions, are very similar, if not the same. What alters is rather the focus of our attention, and part of this is the mere scale of the theatres we will be working in. The same, of course, applies to our next subject – opera.

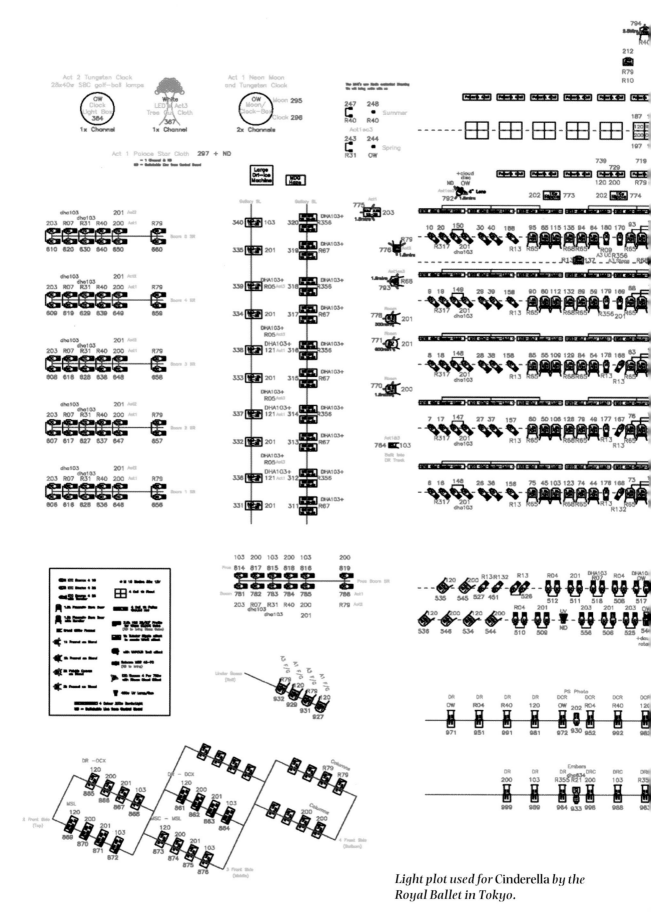

Light plot used for Cinderella *by the Royal Ballet in Tokyo.*

Act2
Act3

284 283
282   281
R09 R79   R40 200

188 181
156 R79
200 075
195 191

734 714
724   704
120 200   R79 R04

Summer
248 245
R40   R40

Act1ac3

Spring
242 241
OW   R31

These Units are are Built into the fireplace
Can you please supply the SEPAL smoke machine

R20/R21/R25
751

R25 ▸741
R21 ▸731
R20 ▸721   Slik
156
RT12 701

Act 1&3 Fireplace

Spaceball
Smoke
Machine
non—dim

5x Channels
3x Non Dim
non—dim

Le Maitre Flash   Mini-Mist Smoke   HDG Haze   Large Dri-Ice Machine

202   873   202   585 585 580 575
R25 200 R79 OW

5 175 92 82 133113 91 81   155 35 25   145   15 5
6   R65 R88 R65   R13   201 R317
R09   dha103

584 579 574
200 R79 OW

DHA103+ R358 310   103 330
DHA103+ R67 309   201 325

R79 L.Centre 878
R88 L.Centre 693
Act1ac3

4 174 87 57 130110 86 56   158 34 24   144   14 4
R356   R88 R65   R13   201 R317
dha103

583 578 573
200 R79 OW

DHA103+ R356 308   Act3 R05 329
DHA103+ R57 307   201 324

DHA103+ Act3 R05

3 173 82 52 127107 81 51   153 33 23   143   13 3
R13 R65 R88 R65   R13   201 R317
dha103

582 577 572
200 R79 OW

DHA103+ R356 306   Act1 121 328
DHA103+ R57 305   201 323

DHA103+ Act3 R05

2 172 77 47 124104 76 46   152 32 22   142   12 2
R13 R65 R88 R65   R13   201 R317
dha103

581 576 571
200 R79 OW

DHA103+ R356 304   Act1 121 326
DHA103+ R87 303   201 322

DHA103+ Act3 R05

1 171 72 42 121101 71 41   151 31 21   141   11 1
R13 R65 R88 R65   R13   201 R317
dha103

DHA103+ R356 302   Act1 121 326
DHA103+ R87 301   201 321

Gallery SL   Gallery SL

Act2 201   dha103
Act1 200 R40 R31 R07 203
Booms 5 SL   R79
655   845 835 825 815 605

Act2 201   dha103
Act1 200 R40 R31 R07 203
Booms 4 SL   R79
854   844 834 624 814 604

Act2 201   dha103
Act1 200 R40 R31 R07 203
Booms 3 SL   R79
853   843 833 623 813 603

Act2 201   dha103
Act1 200 R40 R31 R07 203
Booms 2 SL   R79
652   642 832 622 612 602

Act2 201   dha103
Act1 200 R40 R31 R07 203
Booms 1 SL   R79
651   841 631 621 611 801

DHA103 203 201 R04   203 203   200 120
R35   201   522 521   482 532

Bar 2

RD4 203   201 RD4   200 120 200 120
UV ND
505 553   502 501   481 533 483 531

Bar 1

200 103 200 103 200 103
809   806 808 805 807 804 Pros
Pros Boom SL

Act1 586   685 584 683 582 581 Booms

Act2 R79   200 R40 R31 R07 203
201   dha103

Smoke String Set-up

DL DCL DCL   OP Photo DL   DL
R40 120   OW OW R04   R40 120
993 983   974 923 954   994 984
No 1 Ceiling

GAM Fire/Fx
DLC   DL   DL   DL
R355 106   103   R355
777 200
962 920 998   988   961
No 2 Ceiling

A1 F/G A3 F/G A1 F/G A3 F/G
120 R79 120
R79   922 921
926 924

Under Booms
(Red)

Columns R79 R79
DL — DCX
120
R79
201 200
843 842
Columns
200   200
844

103 201
855 856

3 Front Slide
(Middle)

120
201 200
853 854

MSC — MSR

DL — DCX
120
103 201 200
847
848
MSR
120
200 201
850 849

3 Front Slide
(Top)

DL — DCX
200 120
845
201 846
848

103 201 200
851 852

4 Front Slide
(Bottom)

Cinderella Bunka Kaikan
Toer Van Schaijk
Mark Jonathan
7-8-05

14 LIGHTING FOR OPERA

The process of lighting for opera appears to follow many of the same rules as for lighting drama; however, on closer analysis it is actually a completely different skill. For the professional it is also a much harder discipline. Many lighting designers graduate to opera from lighting prominent works – such as those of Shakespeare – for the major theatres. And of course it is no coincidence that much of the canon has been raided for opera librettos. Works such as *Macbeth*, *Othello* and *Hamlet* offer the breadth of plot, scope of location, and range of dramatic fiction (comic or tragic) required to create a great operatic work.

Opera, both as a form of enjoyment for an audience and in its scope of work for a design team, usually pitches high intellectual goals and extended concepts over a, quite often, long night in the theatre. What opera can also give you, courtesy of some of the largest budgets found in the theatre, is plenty of money and equipment to work with in realizing these ambitions. With expense rarely spared, working in opera can be a designer's dream – but along with the large purse comes an even higher expectation, and the creative bar is accordingly raised high.

An effective lighting designer for opera (as with any form) can be seen as a dependable and indispensable tool for the director/producer, such that they can rest assured that if they employ a particular lighting designer then they know the production will look good. Such a feeling of being guaranteed success in this area will obviously ease part of the concern in undertaking a large challenge. This can also, of course, be applied to all

OPPOSITE: *The Weisbaden Opera House.*

levels of the top theatre institutions, and as a result there can be said to be a 'first division' of designers and lighting designers all able to deliver for the corresponding top league of directors. An opera lighting designer in this situation can see their circuit of work extend certainly across Europe, and more than likely America also. Opera is where you can make your best living as a lighting designer – that is, without courting the commercial sector.

THE SCOPE OF OPERA

Perhaps the ultimate operatic challenge is Wagner's *Ring Cycle*, not everyone's favourite perhaps, but still, in many minds, the ultimate work. Wagner himself was very aware of the theatrical in his work, and went to great lengths in his theatre at Bayreuth to add architectural features to enhance performance. One such was to conceal the orchestra in order to create a more convincing moving real-life vista before the audience – a kind of cinemascope effect before its time. Another innovation was to install hard benches rather than plush seats, arguing that it would force people to pay attention and concentrate on the music!

It is from the former of these two points that we see a part of what an opera director is trying to achieve – perhaps not truly cinemascopic, but nevertheless the realization of a panorama or series of very beautiful stage pictures – even, if you like, stage paintings. Certainly the concept of recreating and bringing to life the works of great master painters is not far from the ambition of many opera producers. Or, in the case of more contemporary pieces, other modern artists can be ransacked for ideas and the piece deliberately created 'in the style of': Salvador Dali, David Hockney, and even the political cartoonist Gerald Scarfe have all seen

The final scene of the Royal Opera's Magic Flute. *Lighting by Paule Constable.*

their work on stage as part of an operatic setting. It is thus often a clear goal in opera to aspire to be a 'high art' form. It is also one of the reasons why, in all the florid architecture of the European opera houses, there is often a gold proscenium – literally a gold picture frame – inside which the richly brought to life, highly visual work can be contained and allowed to flourish.

The German Opera Style

High German standards, as those initially perpetrated at Bayreuth, not only exist in the raw form of opera itself, but also in the technical aspects of the work. German engineering has built many of the world's great opera houses, and refined the stage machinery within it. The history of production and technique has provided us with the basic lighting

style for opera. Imagine dramatic scenes where someone may be singing in a dungeon, and a door is finally opened; or possibly an eclipse taking place, or a climactic sunrise at the end of an act. All such situations call for dramatic lighting moments, and they need power. Should the sun break through clouds and send down powerful arteries of light, we need to be able to see the wonder of this realized within the theatre space.

The German presentational style has used this idea of the sun, or of direction of light source. And reproducing the effect of a natural *single* source, whether the sun or the moon, has necessitated in the German mind the development of increasingly powerful lighting instruments for the theatre. It is also common in the film industry to use high-powered light sources, and in opera the lantern

The Royal Opera's **Magic Flute.** *The crescent moon is a large lighting piece that sits in front of the night sky, which is painted on plastic. The reflection is seen on the floor.*

of choice for this effect is the HMI. This is a remarkable instrument that uses as its source the brilliance of an arcing spark of light (*see* page 69). The colour temperature of the light is matched to daylight, and with current technology the 2.5K and 4K HMI fresnel units are used as main wash instruments. The French company *Robert Juliat* has also developed the HMI profile unit, and has added to our equipment list motorized, digitally controlled shutter sets for the otherwise undimmable fresnels.

THE OPERA RIG

Using large HMI sources to style a rig has evolved in the European theatres of sole opera repertoire, and involves therefore the use of overhead lighting bars with few but powerful instruments. Whether HMI or tungsten, these fixtures can also be fitted with automated yokes and scrollers (*see* page 71). A typical opera rig can consist of perhaps two or three bars, with toplight and backlight being the most important dramatic angles. And of course having fewer LX bars allows for increased grid space for scenery.

To bring light in from front-of-house it is usual for the lighting bridge, sitting just upstage of the proscenium, to be an enormous structure, and have the ability to track a distance up- and downstage; for example, the lighting bridge at the opera house in Helsinki has about six levels, and the higher the levels get, the more they cantilever upstage to enable the lights to see downstage. Such a bridge can have anything and everything rigged on it. Extending down either side of the bridge, and making the structural downstage portal, are the 'tormentor towers' (*see* page 152). They often contain three levels of profiles and PCs, and can also accommodate projectors and other units for specials or effects. The whole of this bridge and tormentor arrangement is then usually clad in a black material to create the so-called 'black pros'; this is then used as a black masking frame inside that of the theatre's gold auditorium proscenium.

The Opera Schedule

The manner in which time is divided in an opera schedule can often present difficulties for the lighting designer. It would seem an only too common and perpetual issue for each opera company house not to have enough time available to match its ambitions for the look and scale of a production. And a repertory opera house can have up to four productions performing at any one time.

It is also true that, unlike dramatic theatre where a production process involves a lighting designer attending a single focus and then plotting session, in opera the fact that rehearsals take place on stage, and usually with a full set, means that, after an initial plot, the lighting designer is expected to use such rehearsals to continue the process. These opportunities to create, recreate, refine, develop and change the lighting come at regular intervals, but over a longer time period than a theatre lighting designer would be used to.

The schedule takes as its starting point the fact that opera singers are generally not required to perform on consecutive nights, and therefore a system of rehearsals in the morning and performances in the evening has evolved. This requires the constant putting in and taking out of productions – allowing for the rehearsal (where a whole set will often be put on stage) and performance of shows – and creates a virtual opera production line.

An opera lighting department deals with this by having a crew available to have a show focused and ready for the beginning of rehearsal at approximately 11a.m. The rehearsal will usually run for something like three hours, and this is also the lighting designer's lighting time for the day. Prior to the sequence of morning rehearsals, there will probably be two technical days to set the focus and build initial cues, and potentially another day halfway through rehearsal time when notes can be caught up on and changes made.

So, within often daunting time constraints for all, a lighting designer has to be aware of what the available lighting kit is, and has to be able to order it to be rigged and de-rigged efficiently and swiftly, or they will not see their designed ideas on stage. The result of this can also lead to the need for immediate lighting ideas and solutions, and hence the technology of large moving light sources, and the philosophy of using them for flexibility and lighting options, has transferred into modern opera houses as a valuable method of lighting productions.

The freedom for ideas that require time occurs in the European theatres, which are more often than not state subsidized. The enforced repertoire of rolling productions to create profit is negated, and a theatre can work on one show at a time. In this situation the set is then built over weeks, in situ on stage, and the growth of a lighting design can be similarly gradual with it. Lighting consequently becomes more integrated into the fabric of a set, whether through conventional means or by the use of architectural fittings, and fluorescent, neon or other such lighting fixtures – or even through the building of lighting units into areas and parts of scenery you could not contemplate using in other circumstances. Some of the European shows have a technical detail and ambition difficult to match, and they approach near-real architectural structures in complexity and detail. Many of the Paris Chatalet shows demonstrate this, as does the floating opera festival in Bregenz, which has recently offered dauntingly huge sets in order to make the operatic lake spectacle bigger and more impressive than ever.

Opera: Lighting the Music

It is, of course, a matter of personal taste as to how one carries out or approaches a lighting design. The opera lighting designer's specific starting point is usually the score, because a good knowledge of the score in turn means you know as much as possible about the libretto, and the structure of the music. You learn the meter of events, and can plan how you will get in and out of scenes, as well as how you will construct the lighting for the scenes themselves. You frequently see a lighting designer's score book laced with well thumbed and moved bookmarks and sticky notes, alongside dividers to identify moments, acts and specific cue points. The music naturally also greatly informs the timing of cues.

A good set designer will produce a storyboard, and between themselves and the director will have a very clear idea of the visual progress of a piece. As lighting designer you should also glean exactly what the vision for the piece is. When sitting down to light you have to remember that merely providing general cover or a wash of light is not usually enough for an opera, because you are lighting a scene moment by moment and creating a real environment on stage for this transported location, wherever it may be.

Follow-spots

Frequently in opera follow-spots are employed, and a good operator is able to light a singer without letting too much light fall on to the scenery behind. Usually, with three or four 'spots' running in a show, all the principals can be highlighted and visually lifted out of the scene. Sometimes they can be just 'glowed' (rising higher for their arias). In addition, a 'spot' operator will fade off altogether when a singer turns upstage, or walks behind a pillar to reappear the other side, or when walking through parts of a set. The task of the follow-spot operator in opera is often an arduous one, where you have to concentrate all the time, and the iris and level are constantly changing for subtlety and not for 'show'. The real skill is for the audience not to know the spot is there.

TOSCA BY PUCCINI FOR THE ROYAL OPERA HOUSE, COVENT GARDEN

To illustrate this kind of detail in opera lighting we can look to **Franco Zefferelli**'s production of Puccini's *Tosca*, a famous production that until recently has been in the repertoire since the early 1960s. The lighting underwent various changes, particularly through the need to use newer equipment over the years, but the essence of the lighting ideas remained intact. The original lighting design was by **William Bundy**, at that time the chief electrician for the Royal Opera, and updated by **John B. Read.**

ACT 1

The first act is the interior of the church of Santa Andrea della Valle in Rome. There is a downstage right structure of pillars, and further off right is the Attavanti small side chapel. Downstage left are iron gates leading to a transept, with two votive candles and a painting above. Between the pillars is a wooden scaffolding rostra for the portrait of Mary Magdalene that Cavaradossi is working on.

All the scenery is made of painted canvas covering wooden pillars or rostra. There is also a backcloth painted to give a distance view of the knave, with arches and windows. The shafts of light painted into the backcloth come in at a high to low angle, and from stage left to right. The area downstage of the pillars is the main playing space of the set, with the pews used by the chorus later in the act.

As an audience member, when you observe the travel of the light through the detail and painting of the set, it appears to pass from stage left to stage right, following a single direction. This sits well with the eye, and completes the stage picture effectively. This was not done by chance, but from good design aesthetics, and by clear and skilled observation. It was scenery built to classic old theatre standards with the use of cleats, lines and braces; and as the production aged, in the way of a grand old master, it gained more integrity with each revival, as another great performance seeps into the cracks. Shows will probably not be designed or built like this again!

As the curtain rises on stage we already have a complete scene, with light painted into it; the lighting designer has to decide how to further evoke the scene. The direction of the light is already there, but how bright should the general ambience of the scene be, and how is the illusion of the church interior to be recreated; for example, the shafts of light on the cloth look bright, but will that be reflected in the light level for the scenes? How is the light in the scenery physically reproduced on stage?

When refocusing and recreating the lighting for *Tosca*, what became apparent was how light was placed into the space to light areas for people – the pews, and around the font downstage right; and then also how light was used to glance across the set – for example, profiles from the downstage stage-left gallery shine down and across the stage-right pillars. Light hitting any of the scenery from a direct front angle is kept to an absolute minimum: in other words, the lighting designer has put light into the scene without needing to simply push in light from the front. It is a delicate approach, which enabled details in the set to be lit beautifully.

Front light is notorious for flattening a stage picture, and is usually the opposite of what is required when lighting an opera set. We may know that we are not really looking at a marble pillar, but we do not want to actually see whether it is a thing of plaster and paint, or a painted cloth.

Tosca in the final moments of Act II. Note the shadows from the fire and the pool of light from the candles.

The windows on the backcloth for Act 1 are backlit with profiles, the cloth front lit originally by a single Patten 49 (an old Strand 1000w 120° flood) hidden behind the set upstage right of centre. The light for the downstage area is keyed in through the gates on stage left, and washes across into the pews and up to the painting platform. General light is pushed in from the stage-right perch, but in L201 (tungsten to daylight colour conversion, *see* page 30), offering a darker shade to the open white from stage left, and not competing with the effect of direction.

The whole of the scenery has specials picking out details: for example, a top light on the Madonna downstage left. The painting of the Madonna itself has three specials, two recreating shafts of light glancing across the front, and a single unit to highlight the head in the portrait.

Thus the lighting recreates the church interior, and the singers and chorus play in this light as details of the scene – as living members of the painting we are looking at. When more light is required, there is a direct special from a front-of-house position or from the perch, which offers a better dramatic angle since it is more side on.

ACT 2

In Act 2 the scene has shifted to Scarpia's chamber at the Farnese Palace. Cavaradossi is to be held prisoner in the basement to extort information on Angelotti from Tosca. A floorcloth with a black-and-white perspective panelled design mimicking marble tiles, was put down in the interval. Once the flats are run in to create the room, all is set, and the focal point of the room is a large fireplace mid-stage right. The walls formed a box set that has two borders overhead, up-and-down side borders, and no overhead lighting. The principal lighting source has therefore become the fireplace itself.

Unknown to the audience, behind the fireplace sits a complex setting of lighting units to create the effect of the flames of the fire lighting the room. Fire-effects projectors (notoriously poor in light output) were not used for this, as the lighting called for an effect altogether more powerful. If the fireplace is to light the room, you need to have the lighting levels of standard instruments, and for a figure to stand lit by the flames you also need to recreate the effect of the flickering light licking around the people and the room. In all, what is required for this act is that you use light to create a dramatic, lascivious heaviness underpinning the politics of the scene and Scarpia's deviant manoeuvrings.

For the fire effect, a piece of silk was taken, fixed to a frame, then cut vertically to create ribbons that were held in place top and bottom. Air from a fan was then blown across the ribbons and, with a light positioned just behind projecting through the silk, the image of the flickering light was projected through the opening of the fire to whatever lay beyond. The clever part of this lighting effect was that the fans also had barndoors, so the rate of flicker could be adjusted, hence creating an exact effect. Within the fireplace lighting rig there were lamps that focused straight across on to the opposite stage-left set wall, and a particular single fresnel, with its own fan, to shoot on to the doors upstage centre where Tosca stood dramatically holding a final position at the end of the act. L134 (golden amber) was used for the fire, a bold choice, but nevertheless a colour that so communicated exactly what was intended that you did not ask questions as to why the colour or what the source.

There are two fine lighting moments contained in Act 2 of *Tosca* involving the character of Spoleta, one of Scarpia's spies. The first is when the trap door opens downstage left of centre, and he stands upstage of the opening peering over. Underneath the stage for this, a 2K fresnel was placed on a bench-base (a short stand) and focused up through the hatch, and a Patt 23 (500W fixed-beam profile) on a 2ft stand. The 2K sat at the base of the stairs under the stage, and was spotted-down, lifted and angled so that it could see over the set walls avoiding the stage-right up-and-down border. It was also nudged downstage enough to stay off the scenic border overhead. The Patt 23 was focused directly for Spoleta's face, but also positioned to keep the light off the overhead border. The lights are in use in the cue when the hatch is opened, but cannot be seen, and this careful focus has to be checked every time prior to the show. The gel used is again Lee 134, and, for the moment when Spoleta peers over, the singer learnt exactly how to let his face fall into the light as he surveys Cavaradossi held below.

The second clever lighting moment in this act is very similar. When Spoleta stands by the fireplace there is plenty of light contained within the scene, but none, as such, covering up to his face height. The solution is to place a small fresnel on the floor behind the fire, which kicked up again off the border specifically to catch Spoleta's face. As a member of the audience you would not know this, and it works so perfectly that you happily accept that he is being lit by the glow of the flames.

Act 3

The setting for Act 3 is the Santa Angelo Castle, where Cavaradossi is awaiting the firing squad and writes a letter to Tosca. The scene famously used a wrap-around cyclorama that took half an hour to hand-winch round from downstage right; it was seamless and went to a staggering height. It presented a genuine panorama – a vault of air giving a real impression of the sky and distance over the castle walls. The original bar to light this 'cyc' was called the Main 'Cyc' and had a barrage of Patten 49 units rigged on it. Lee 132 (medium blue) was used for the blue, chosen in an age when there were no other shades of deep blue available. It was, and remains, perfectly sound as a colour to use, just as Lee 103 (straw) is still a perfectly decent amber – some clichés are simply clichés because they are right! The battens sitting further upstage are trimmed at increasing heights to remain out of view, and also use the Lee 132 from the standard ballet border light units (*see* page 156) to wash upstage and complete the 'cyc' cover.

The extent of the realism in the setting extended to the 'stars', suspended once again on special winches from the grid, and which, once in position, correspond to the actual constellation you would have seen in the Italian night sky! Layered on top of the blue are clouds projecting from the lower bridge.

The magic moment in this act occurs at the end, and involves various cues for dawn, all of which have different timings in order to account for differing intensities seen on the 'cyc' over the differing heights of the set, as it is brilliantly silhouetted against the rising sun. The effect is further enhanced by the gradual introduction of Lee 109 (light salmon), coming only from below in the final closing moments before the tabs come in.

CONTEMPORARY OPERA LIGHTING DESIGN

Zefferelli's *Tosca* has a set with the detail painted on to the scenery, the style of which rarely gets seen or constructed today. There has been a generation of designers since – such as **Michael Yeargen** and **Richard Hudson** – who have introduced the interplay of flat planes, of surfaces and colour into their work, and have developed a new look and standard for opera scenery. With building techniques and drafting for modern scenery done on CAD programs, a straight line in the theatre is now true and absolute, and this precision is communicated into the final look of a set so that contemporary opera designs tend to have a much more precise architecture. This feature evolved throughout the 1990s as theatre companies acquired the computer power and know-how to realize it.

The style of a set can also transfer into the style of the lighting, which nowadays uses precision where there possibly used to be more subtlety in mood. This goes hand in hand with a style of lighting derived from a set of particular instruments. *Tosca* lighting sources were completely tungsten, even the projectors; it is interesting, therefore, to compare equipment used for a recent production of *Bluebeard* for the Royal Opera (lighting by David Finn), and the production of *Tosca* described above (the list for *Tosca* shows the equipment used to reproduce the lighting as described in the text on page 167 onwards): *see* list opposite.

These two productions represent equipment used at the Royal Opera before the redevelopment in 1996, and that of the new theatre opened in 1999. The two shows are, of course, very different in style, which is precisely the point of the illustration – this is how far the modern vocabulary of opera lighting equipment has developed in order to effectively take it into a new realm of staging, both in terms of set and lighting. The range of tungsten units has dramatically reduced, the range of British lighting kit has almost expired, and the new units are extremely diverse in power and application.

Now, an HMI fresnel source is not being used to pierce through a rig as a wash of real daylight, it is being used as a shade of coloured light in its own right. HMI has a power, a harshness and a clinicality to pour on to and over the similarly huge constructions of a modern opera setting. The development of HMI profiles means a whole rig can now be based around discharge sources, and then tungsten can be introduced as a warmer, gentler source – indeed, the role of HMI could be said to have so changed that it is now sometimes the predominant light source.

Of course, all designers are different, and **Paule Constable**, while giving herself a colour palette of largely Lee warm and cold correction filters, in the main sticks to using tungsten, and in particular the parcan and the fresnel in her work. The irony of this, when describing present opera lighting, is that in an era when others use obscure light sources and technology, the stamp of Constable's work has gained a very successful foothold in the industry. She has a style that can by no means be called 'traditional'.

Summary

The mere scale of much opera work can bring enormous rewards to the lighting designer, and yet it remains embedded in all the principles that we have already discussed in the earlier chapters of this book. For in the end, light remains light, and the basic ideas behind how we use it remain just as valid whether applied to drama, dance or opera.

Opera lighting equipment in 2006 compared to 1996

Bluebeard

Lantern	# of Units
Source 4 19°	22
Source 4 19° Moving Yoke	12
Source 4 26°	32
Source 4 36°	4
Source 4 50°	5
1.2K Profile	3
Par64 CP62	16
Selecon 90°	4
2.5K Fresnel	13
2.5K PC	2
Studio Colour Moving Head	8
150W Flood	5
Iris 1 Flood	20
2.5K HMI Fresnel	8
4K HMI Moving Yoke	1
Mini–Brute	1
2K Blonde Fresnel	4
HMI Profile	7
M16 75W	15
Fibre Optic Box	1
M16 50W	12
10K Fresnel	2
4K HMI Fresnel	1
Orion Groundrow	16
Svoboda Light Curtain	5 metres
5K Fresnel	3
ACL Parcans	8
Fluorescent 5ft 2 Way Battens	37

Tosca

Lantern	# of Units
Source 4 26°	8
Sil 30°	18
Patt 293 Profile	9
Cantata 1–2K Profile	21
Berkey 2K Fresnel	6
Altman Leko 6×12	2
Harmony 1K Profile	17
Teatro 1K Profile	32
Patt 49 Flood	1
ADB 2K Fresnel	1
Pageant Beamlight	10
Patt 23 Profile	1
Minuette Fresnel	1
1K Fresnel	4
Cantata 1–2K Fresnel	1
Patt 137 Flood	2
Patt 52 Projector	3
Berkey Groundrow	8

ENDNOTE

The ideas in this book have been arrived at through practice and experience. The underlying thought throughout has been to be aware, be clear, be organized, and be quick.

You can only be a designer, of any description, if you have the kind of mind that can create ideas, and in lighting these ideas come just as much from an awareness of what is around us every day as from our own imagination. Applying these ideas to the technical arena is a unique combination of the creative and the practical, the artistic and the technical, and one in which we only grow and develop with practice. Good technical knowledge is then only applied well if our concepts are clear and as simple as possible. As with all art forms, and as has been repeated throughout this book, *less is always more.*

The usual race against time – the adhering to a production schedule oppressed by the concept that 'time is money' – requires clarity and pace. All of this can be exhausting, but the rewards – the satisfaction of a job well done – as in every artistic endeavour, are high.

The final point therefore to make at the end of this guide is that the process of lighting for any kind of theatre performance should, on the majority of occasions (it is a job, after all), be both creatively fulfilling and, most importantly, highly enjoyable. At a practical level the work can be hard, the hours long and (usually) the pay fairly meagre. It is important therefore that we find our rewards in the challenges of the process, in having done a job well, and in taking our own share of the applause that should accompany success.

And 'should' is in the sentence above because an element of luck is essential to the artistic endeavour of producing a work on stage. The lighting designer is only a part of the process and cannot, indeed need not, worry about every aspect of the overall concept – the director and producers can worry about that – and the critics and the paying public. It is therefore important that we set our own standards for our work and know how well we, and our lighting, is doing. We must be our own severest critic, and learn to take our own notes, and work to our own satisfaction as appropriate – to do the job to the best of our ability, and then move on.

The authors of this book wish you more than your fair share of good luck as lighting designers, and hope that this guide will have been of some use as you continue in your (it is to be hoped) brilliant endeavours to design with light.

BIBLIOGRAPHY

Bell, R., *Let there be Light – Entertainment Lighting Software Pioneers in Conversation* (Entertainment Technology Press, 2004)

Cadena, R., *Focus on Lighting Technology* (Entertainment Technology Press, 2002)

Colman, P., *Basics – A Beginner's Guide to Special Effects* (Entertainment Technology Press, 2005)

Fitt, B., *A–Z of Lighting Terms* (Focal Press, 1999)

Fraser, N., *Lighting & Sound*, 2nd edition (Phaidon Press, 1991)

Fraser, N., *Stage Lighting Design – A Practical Guide* (Crowood, 1999)

Fraser, N., *Stage Lighting Explained* (Crowood, 2002)

Morgan, N. H., *Stage Lighting Design in Britain: The Emergence of the Lighting Designer, 1881–1950* (Entertainment Technology Press, 2005)

Morgan, N. H., *Stage Lighting for Theatre Designers* (Entertainment Technology Press, 2003)

Pilbrow, R., *Stage Lighting Design – The Art, The Craft, The Life* (Nick Hern Books, 1997)

Rees, T., *Theatre Lighting in the Age of Gas* (The Society for Theatre Research, 1978)

Reid, F., *The ABC of Stage Lighting* (A&C Black, 1992)

Reid, F., *Discovering Stage Lighting* (Focal Press, 1993)

Reid, F., *Lighting the Stage* (Focal Press, 1995)

Reid, F., The *Stage Lighting Handbook*, 5th edition (A&C Black, 1996)

Schiller, B., *The Automated Lighting Programmer's Handbook* (Focal Press, 2004)

Shelley, S. L., *A Practical Guide to Stage Lighting* (Focal Press, 1999)

Simpson, R. S., *Lighting Control – Technology and Applications* (Focal Press, 2003)

Staines, J., *Lighting Techniques for Theatre-in-the-Round* (Entertainment Technology Press, 2000)

Streader, T., and Williams, J., *Create Your Own Stage Lighting* (Bell & Hymen, 1985)

Walne, G. (ed.), *Effects for the Theatre* (A&C Black, 1995)

Warfel, W. B., *The New Handbook of Stage Lighting Graphics* (Nick Hern Books, 2001)

INDEX

PHOTO CREDITS